REVOLUTIONS

OF THE *MIND*

Cultural Studies
in the *African Diaspora Project*
1996-2002

CAAS Publications
Ralph J. Bunche Center for African American Studies at UCLA
[Formerly the UCLA Center for African American Studies (CAAS)]
160 Haines Hall
Box 951545
University of California, Los Angeles 90095

Library of Congress Cataloging-in-Publication Data

Revolutions of the mind : Cultural Studies in the African Diaspora
Project, 1996-2002 / edited by Dionne Bennett . . . [et al.] ; CSADP
conceived by Valerie Smith and Marcyliena Morgan.
p. cm.
Includes bibliographical references.
ISBN 0-934934-47-9 (alk. paper)
1. Cultural Studies in the African Diaspora Project. 2. African
Americans–Research–United States. 5. African Americans–Study and
teaching (Higher)–United States. 6. Blacks–Study and teaching
(Higher)–United States. 7. African diaspora–Study and teaching
(Higher)–United States. 8. African Americans–Intellectual life. 9.
Blacks–Intellectual life. I. Bennett, Dionne. II. Smith, Valerie, 1956- III.
Morgan, Marcyliena H. IV. Cultural Studies in the African Diaspora
Project.
E184.7.R47 2003
973'.0496073'0072–dc21
                                                      2003002725

ISBN: 0-934934-47-9

Senior Editor, CAAS Publications: Ulli K. Ryder
Editor, CAAS Publications: Candace Moore
Editorial Assistant, CAAS Publications: Erin Randolph

Designed by Candace Moore
Front and back cover art from original artwork by Branyon Davis

www.bunchecenter.ucla.edu

REVOLUTIONS

OF THE *MIND*

Cultural Studies
in the African Diaspora Project
1996-2002

Edited by
**Dionne Bennett, Candace Moore,
Ulli K. Ryder,** and **Jakobi Williams**

CSADP conceived by
Valerie Smith and **Marcyliena Morgan**
Funded by **The Ford Foundation**

ACKNOWLEDGMENTS

Sincere thanks to Valerie Smith, Marcyliena Morgan, Darnell Hunt, Claudia Mitchell-Kernan, Richard Yarborough, Nandini Gunewardena, and Mark Sawyer for their dedicated service as advisors, mentors, administrators, and role models to the Cultural Studies in the African Diaspora Project (CSADP). Thanks also to the CSADP advisory board, as well as the UCLA Center for African American Studies (now the Ralph J. Bunche Center for African American Studies at UCLA) staff members who have assisted the Diaspora Project over the course of its six years, most notably Management Services Officer Jan Freeman.

A special thanks to the Ford Foundation and to Ford Foundation Program Officers Margaret Wilkerson and Gertrude J. Fraser whose support and encouragement allowed the vision of the CSADP to be realized.

The exhaustive efforts of all of the members of the CSADP staff over the project's tenure produced the events documented here, made this publication possible, and cannot be thanked enough.

TABLE OF CONTENTS

PREFACE

CLAUDIA MITCHELL-KERNAN

We can better understand African Americans by understanding Africans and those of African descent everywhere. In the simplest language, this is the motivating insight of the scholars whose work on the African Diaspora fills this volume. This insight found expression throughout the twentieth century in works such as W.E.B. Du Bois's *Black Folk Then and Now: An Essay in the History and Sociology of the Negro Race* (1941) and St. Clair Drake's *Black Folk Here and There: An Essay in History and Anthropology* (Vol. 1, 1987; Vol. II, 1990). It was also memorialized in the content and organization of the *Journal of Negro History* from its inception in 1916.

More important in the scheme of concerns that have been central to me, we cannot understand the social and political inequalities that continue to stand as a barrier to both peace and progress without understanding the forces that created the African Diaspora, forces that sent millions of people away from their ancestral homeland to build new communities in the Caribbean, Europe, and North and South America.

As we sit in the United States in the twenty-first century, these may sound like relatively mundane statements. The burgeoning field of African American studies, after all, is now decades old, and we have all enjoyed the fruits of those who labored to create it. Moreover, the legacies in political economy and ideology of the colonial and imperial era are sufficiently documented that we can assess the era's impact from the point of view of the colonized as well as the colonizers. This was not always so, however.

As some find it easy today to accept America's world dominance as a force that fosters democracy and does no harm, or to see homeless people as victims of their own unwillingness to work, there was a time and place when slavery seemed a useful economic arrangement and colonizing countries seemed the bearers of true religion and culture. One of the gifts of growing older is to see how "truths" change as time passes.

When I began my work in anthropology in the 1960s, the discipline still reflected traditions that were established at the beginning of the twentieth century and in force until at least 1920. Despite some changes in the 1940s and 1950s, anthropologists continued to focus mostly on what they called small-scale societies. They asked questions about those societies that I still find interesting today: How did societies come to be as they are? How can a society be adequately described? How does one society differ from another?

While the questions were sound, however, the process of answering them was undermined by the fact that research in anthropology was frequently conducted as if European hegemony did not exist. The literature on Africa and other parts of the world described people who were frozen in time, viewed in some magical way that prevented them from knowing they were observed and wondering who the observers were. Their cultures were treated like museum pieces: By simply observing a village, researchers thought they could understand it completely. Worldwide political, economic, and social changes—those forces that people now collectively call globalization—were considered irrelevant.

I suppose I was particularly sensitive to these defects in the research process because my family traced its origins to Africa—one of the places the European researchers had examined from the privileged position of Western elites. Like many African Americans during the 1950s and 1960s, I redirected the course and meaning of my life in both subtle and overt ways as a result of the American Civil Rights Movement. Therefore, early in my education as an anthropologist, events in the political sphere led me to believe that while anthropology's comparative methods had value, anthropological paradigms were characterized by significant deficiencies. Although others were reaching similar conclusions, I was reasoning from a somewhat different perspective: looking at the decolonization of Africa and other parts of the world, and the transformations that resulted from that process.

In fact, because of the political and cultural consciousness-raising that occurred at this time, many of us were seeing things from what came to be known as an African Diaspora perspective. The central ideas were afloat long before the term was found to describe them. From the beginning, African Diaspora research encouraged anthropologists to ask questions that are continuously relevant because the answers change as our knowledge of each other and ourselves grows. What happened to people of African descent in the wake of slavery? Were they all oppressed in the same way? How did their oppression differ in different contexts? How did they live then, and how do they live now? How are they like each other? How are they different and why is that so? Are some more "African" or less "African" than others and what do we mean when we say that? What are the forces that have shaped the lives of different groups throughout the African Diaspora? What are the attitudes that people have about themselves and about those forces? What does it mean that some African Diaspora people were demographically dominant in the places they lived, whereas in the United States, African Americans were a demographic minority? How did all of those things affect what we experience when we travel around the country or walk through our neighborhoods? How do we relate to oppressed people from different Diasporas? How do we build coalitions within and beyond the African

Diaspora? What are the tools used to do African Diaspora research? These questions and many others remain important for us to explore.

As I started to ask myself those questions, the African Diaspora perspective began to influence my approach to anthropology. It did so in stages. Initially, I thought my life would be spent outside of the United States in far-away, "exotic" villages all over the world. That was my goal; that was my idea of "doing anthropology." Anthropologists have historically been invested in the notion that researchers should never study their own culture. When I was being trained, you weren't a "real" anthropologist unless you went off to a different country and studied a rural community, and I certainly appreciate the value of such research. I conducted what some would consider traditional anthropological research in Samoa and learned a great deal there. However, the Civil Rights Movement led me to the realization that I was probably going to find it the most meaningful—in terms of my own intellectual growth and in terms of the larger intellectual projects that interested me—to study African Americans.

I soon discovered that in order to get to an understanding of what happened to people of African descent in the context of the United States, I needed to know a lot more about what Africans were like before they came to the United States. I realized that I had to do research on Africa. I knew that my understanding had to begin to cross boundaries, both geographical and disciplinary.

I began with a focus on language. My reading on Africa profoundly affected my research on African American English and later on creolization in Belize. At the same time, conducting comparative research in two African Diaspora cultures and observing the startling similarities between Belizean and African American speech behavior provided me with compelling evidence of what Melville Herskovits would have called African retentions and reinterpretations. I had read about these, but through research I saw them for myself on the ground in the field.

At UCLA, my focus on the African Diaspora took a new direction. A few years after my arrival, I was appointed Director of the Center for African American Studies. In that role, one of my goals was to develop research, teaching, and publication programs that would turn African Diaspora research into a programmatic direction that not only forged connections between different kinds of theories and research but also encouraged international dialogue among scholars. I supported the Cultural Studies in the African Diaspora Project, which is under the Center's umbrella, in part because I was grateful that others were institutionalizing the African Diaspora perspective. I have always been concerned that the African Diaspora perspective, like many powerful critical tools, would not survive without advocacy.

African Diaspora research is both an intellectual project and a political project. The kinds of questions that are raised by African Diaspora studies, as well as African American studies and all ethnic studies programs, are critical questions for the modern world because they are linked to the larger problematics of inequality. Ultimately, the social sciences, the humanities, and the sciences have to come to a more fundamental understanding of the causes and the consequences of inequality. We must fully understand the costs of inequality not only for individuals and local groups, but for the larger society they compose. Ultimately, there is a cost for everybody.

Looking at things from an African Diaspora perspective contributes to the process of understanding and addressing inequality by giving people, especially people of African descent, a different level of awareness of their situation. Too often we see the world exclusively in terms of the local and the individual. It is critically important to think about the many questions we want to answer in a more transnational context. In some ways, this also speaks to concerns raised by Carter J. Woodson in his *The Miseducation of the Negro* (1933): making black people see things in narrowly local terms was part of the process of their miseducation. The work of the Cultural Studies in the African Diaspora Project, which concludes its six-year mission with this volume, has helped to reverse that process. I welcome its contributions as a scholar of the African Diaspora, as a university administrator who struggles against persistent inequities, and as an individual who has seen great change and wants more.

For me, supporting African Diaspora research and projects that encourage it, like the Cultural Studies in the African Diaspora Project, is a way to honor my belief, not always reinforced, that understanding and knowledge really *are* liberating, and that if you influence what people know, ultimately, you have an impact on what they think, what they believe, and, perhaps, what they will do.

INTRODUCTION:
AN OVERVIEW OF THE CULTURAL STUDIES
IN THE AFRICAN DIASPORA PROJECT

DIONNE BENNETT, DARNELL HUNT,
MARCYLIENA MORGAN, AND VALERIE SMITH

Di·as·po·ra (dI-'as-p ər ə)

Etymology: Greek, from *diaspeirein* to spread about, *dia-* + *speirein* to sow, scatter. The dispersion, migration, and settlement of a people away from their ancestral homelands.

THE CSADP—A NEW BEGINNING
FOR AFRICAN DIASPORA RESEARCH

In the spring of 1996, UCLA Professors Marcyliena Morgan (Anthropology) and Valerie Smith (English) received a three-year grant from the Ford Foundation to establish the Cultural Studies in the African Diaspora Project (CSADP), a research initiative affiliated with the UCLA Center for African American Studies (CAAS). The primary aims of the CSADP were to encourage scholarly activity by and about people of African descent, and to provide a framework to increase collaborative and interdisciplinary research and teaching about the African Diaspora. To this end, the CSADP sponsored annual colloquium series, conferences, interactive media initiatives, and graduate student research.

The CSADP provided a site for conceptualizing new meanings of black identity in the context of changing notions of national identity, global market, and the nation-state in the late-twentieth- and early-twenty-first century. In keeping with the goals of Cultural Studies as a discipline, it both encouraged linkages between policy, humanities, arts, and social science research, and helped to forge new and dynamic connections between cultural production, activism, and research on and off campus.

CSADP colloquia and special events were attended by numerous individuals from the UCLA and wider Los Angeles communities. At a time when politics at the state and national levels threatened the presence of students of color on college and university campuses, and challenged the very existence of ethnic studies programs and departments, these activities helped to heighten the visibility of African American and African Diaspora Studies in Southern California. For example, during its first year, CSADP formed an enduring partnership with KAOS Network, an organization that promotes the artistic expression of inner-city youth in the Leimert Park neighborhood of Los Angeles. Ben Caldwell, the founder and director of KAOS Network, facilitated this collaboration, which was maintained throughout the project.

The value of the experience gained by the graduate students involved in the CSADP cannot be overstated. The CSADP gave students key roles in the planning and execution of its programs, thereby providing opportunities for mentorship and collaborative learning with faculty, both at UCLA and elsewhere. The Diaspora Project office was staffed by graduate students whose duties included research, coordinating events, supervising work-study undergraduate students, maintaining the web site and library collection, and functioning as liaisons with members of the CSADP advisory committee. Student involvement in various colloquium series and conferences was particularly rewarding. This opportunity to dialogue with senior scholars enhanced the intellectual development of students and helped socialize these students into their developing identities as scholars. On a material level, the CSADP was able to provide essential support that ensured that graduate students had the financial resources to continue their academic careers. The CSADP was also able to support numerous research trips and travel to conferences for both graduate students and faculty.

Over the years, with the help of the CSADP, African Diasporic research at UCLA was made increasingly visible locally, nationally, and even internationally. The intention of the project was to create an institutional model that would nurture a complex critical discourse about African peoples and cultures that would be sustained indefinitely. Following is a summary of these efforts to be used not only as a document of the project, but also, we hope, as a suggestive guide for others who seek to continue this essential work.

CSADP—YEAR ONE (1996-1997)

During the first year of the CSADP, the project's primary focus was "Race, Culture, and Citizenship," and encompassed issues of migration, identity, and ethnicity. Not only did this particular topic allow project participants to take up the current debates in the U.S. surrounding African American identity—including affirmative action, restitution, and immigrant rights—but it also provided a context for considering the treatment of citizens and immigrants of African descent in Europe, especially since the formation of the European Community (EC) and the European Economic Union (EEU).

Major objectives of the CSADP involved strengthening local intercampus ties and enhancing intellectual exchange around African American studies–related issues at UCLA. To that end, a colloquium series was established to allow scholars to share their research. During the first year, the colloquium speakers included: Ann duCille, Ruth Wilson Gilmore, bell hooks, Gerald Jaynes, Kobena Mercer, Brenda Stevenson, and Mary Helen Washington.

With help from the UCLA Center for African American Studies, the Dean of Social Sciences, the Dean of Humanities, and the Vice-Chancellor for Academic Affairs, the CSADP sponsored a major conference entitled *Race, Class, and Citizenship: Western Europe and the United States*. The conference was divided into three sessions: "The Politics of Race, Class, Identity, and Immigration"; "Women and the State: Politics and Struggle in Western Europe"; and "Representation and Resistance in Art and Culture."

CSADP—YEAR TWO (1997-1998)

During the second year of the project, the CSADP sponsored a symposium entitled *Put Your Hands Together: Representation, Interpretation, and Black Spirituality* with the UCLA Center for African American Studies and the UCLA Center for the Study of Religion. Scholars presented research on black religious practices in the African Diaspora. Because UCLA does not have a religious studies department, audience members enjoyed having the opportunity to discuss religious issues in a critical context. Speakers for the event included: D. Keith Naylor, Katherine Clay Bassard, and Guthrie Ramsey.

The colloquium series this year continued to explore constructions of race and class as well as the politics of black popular culture. Invited speakers explored ways in which social sciences' and humanities' methodologies might inform and inflect each other. Colloquium speakers included the following: Todd Boyd, Farah Jasmine Griffin, Warren Crichlow, and Leo Spitzer.

The CSADP also presented a lecture and screening of the film *The Watermelon Woman* by director Cheryl Dunye, cosponsored with the UCLA Department of Film and Television; the UCLA Center for the Study of Women; and the Lesbian, Gay, Bisexual, and Transgender Studies

Program at UCLA. The project also awarded support to Abel Valenzuela, Assistant Professor in the UCLA Chavez Center for Chicano Studies, to support the development of a new interdisciplinary course on interethnic relations in urban communities.

CSADP—YEAR THREE (1998-1999)

In its third year, the Diaspora Project turned its focus to the theme "The Arts, Performance and Popular Culture" in response to several unique opportunities for collaboration with other institutions. The Los Angeles County Museum of Art (LACMA) asked the CSADP to develop programming in conjunction with their 1998 exhibition entitled *Rhapsodies in Black: Arts of the Harlem Renaissance*. CSADP worked with David Bailey, a co-curator of the LACMA exhibition, to plan a conference on October 9-10, 1998 entitled *Rhapsodies in Blax: The Harlem Renaissance and the Blaxploitation Movement: 1920-1990s*. The conference sought to expand prevailing notions of both Blaxploitation and the Harlem Renaissance by exploring how the earlier movement paved the way for the later period; how the Blaxploitation movement in cinema informed other visual arts, literature, music and fashion; and how the '70s movement continues to echo in the work of black artists today. The event brought together artists and scholars from the United States and the U.K. and allowed participants to consider the connections between these twentieth century moments of black cultural productivity across a range of genres. *Rhapsodies in Blax* was cosponsored by numerous campus departments and programs as well as by the Peter Norton Family Foundation, which hosted a reception for participants and guests.

Panels for the event included: "Reinventing Histories"; "Gangsterism and Urban Spaces"; and "Redefining Genres: Transgression and Passing." Speakers for the event included: David Bailey, Hazel

Carby, Andres Chavez, Ron Finley, Haile Gerima, Herman Gray, Kellie Jones, Isaac Julien, Marcyliena Morgan, Ngozi Onwurah, Richard J. Powell, Valerie Smith, Armond White, Judith Wilson, Richard Yarborough, Lola Young, and Pauline Yu.

In response to the growing scholarly and extracurricular interest in hip-hop culture, CSADP graduate students organized *Power Moves: A Conference on Hip-hop Culture*. The conference attracted national attention and featured scholars, graffiti artists, performers, and community activists from around the nation. The conference was organized around informal round-table panels and also featured a more formal graduate student symposium, a comprehensive web site, hip-hop films, a live drumming demonstration, and a poetry performance. Its cosponsors included numerous campus departments and programs, as well as Skechers USA.

The conference featured the following panels: "In Visions: Hip-hop Culture and Representation"; "Flip the Script: The Cross-Cultural Transmission of Hip-hop Style, Technique, and Language"; "Ladies First: Women's Voices and Discourses of Gender, Sexism, and Power"; "CHIP$, CHEDDAR AND C.R.E.A.M.: Materialism, Revolutionary Politics, Authorship, Ownership, and 'Selling Out'"; and "Fight the Power: Hip-hop as a Political Youth Movement." Speakers for the event included Rap Artists: Fab 5 Freddy, Ice-T, Tyrin Turner, Medusa, Ras Kass, Boots, Dusk One, DJ Sake One; Filmmakers: Bob Bryan, Thomas Guzman-Sanchez, Ben Caldwell; Graffiti Writers/Visual Artists: Carlos "Mare 139" Rodriguez, WANE, Sandra "Lady Pink" Fabara, SPIE; Author: S.H. Fernando, Jr.; Activists: Hodari Davis, Jasmin Barker, Frank Sosa, Rishi Nath; Radio Personalities: Leslie "Big Lez" Segar, Davey D; Editors: Kierna Mayo and KET; Academics: Craig Watkins, Lakandiwa M. de Leon, Cheryl Keyes, George Lipsitz; Choreographer, Asia; and Poet, Kamau Daaood.

The CSADP also cosponsored a range of events, including the *Alpha Phi Alpha Miss Black and Gold Pageant*; the *50th Anniversary of Black History Month* celebration at the Fowler Museum at UCLA; a book signing and discussion of *The Ties that Bind: Timeless Values for African American Families*, by Joyce Ladner; lectures and screenings by Stanley Nelson and Attallah Shabazz; and lectures by Tricia Rose, Mark Solomon, Florence Bellande-Robertson, and Lilas Dequirons. The CSADP also cosponsored *The Duke Ellington Centennial Conference* hosted principally by the UCLA Department of Ethnomusicology and the UCLA School of the Arts.

CSADP—YEAR FOUR (1999-2000)

Because of the success of the first phase of the project, the CSADP received funds from the Ford Foundation, along with a commitment from UCLA Dean/Vice Chancellor Claudia Mitchell-Kernan (Graduate Division/Graduate Studies), UCLA Dean Scott Waugh (Social Sciences), and UCLA Dean Pauline Yu (Humanities) for a three-year Phase II of the project in 1999. In the first year of Phase II, the Diaspora Project organized a symposium entitled *Memory, Representations, and the Black '60s*, a two-day event organized in conjunction with *Mementos*, an exhibition of the work of Kerry James Marshall, on view at the Santa Monica Museum of Art. In *Mementos*, Marshall explored the impact of public tragedies upon private lives and histories. His multimedia installations created spaces for viewers to confront both the losses and gains associated with the 1960s. For the event, a range of artists and scholars were invited to reflect upon the impact of the racial politics of the 1960s from a variety of perspectives. Invited guests included Elizabeth Abel, Houston Baker, Clayborne Carson, Louis Massiah, and Richard Powell. The event also included a poetry reading featuring Kamau Daaood, Ruth Forman, Ojenke, K.W. Kgositsile, and Quincy Troupe.

The CSADP was able to cosponsor a number of other events during this period. These events included lectures by Vaginal Davis (cosponsored with the UCLA Office of Instructional Development and the Lesbian, Gay, Bisexual, and Transgender Studies Program at UCLA) and Robin D. G. Kelley (cosponsored with the UCLA Oral History Program, the James V. Mink Oral History Lecture Fund, the Interdepartmental Program in Afro-American Studies, and the UCLA Departments of Musicology and Ethnomusicology).

CSADP—YEAR 5 (2000-2001)

In January 2001, the CSADP cosponsored *The African Presence in the Spanish and Lusophone World*. This international conference was organized by Professor Mark Sawyer and included participants from several Latin American countries. Panels included: "Blacks and Racism in the Spanish and Portuguese World: Racial Attitudes Examined"; "The Myth of Racial Democracy and Black Political Advancement"; and "Black Culture and Consciousness in Latin America." In addition to bringing together remarkable scholars from all over the world, the conference issued a call for the recognition of Latin America as a critical site for African Diaspora research and of the meaningful cultural, historical, and intellectual bonds shared by black and Latino communities that warrant exploration and celebration.

The CSADP also sponsored a two-day conference, *A Love Supreme: Romance, Sexuality, Friendship, and Family in the African Diaspora*, between February 9-10, 2001. Events included a poetry reading and film festival; presentations by graduate students from several universities; a round-table discussion on black romance in the media; informative and inspiring keynote addresses by Professors Brenda E. Stevenson and

James H. Cones, III; and a discussion of Cheryl Dunye's film *The Watermelon Woman* led by Professor Mary Helen Washington.

CSADP—YEAR 6 (2001-2002)
FINAL YEAR

In 2001-2002, the CSADP formed bonds with a national roster of scholars through *The Third World Re-order Lecture Series in Honor of Claudia Mitchell-Kernan*. This monthly speaker series featured an interdisciplinary group of scholars and celebrated the contributions made by Dr. Claudia Mitchell-Kernan, both to African Diaspora Research in general and to the CSADP and its unique achievements. Lectures addressed how twenty-first century members of African communities learn from their pasts, address current challenges, and prepare for impending struggles and victories.

In 2002, the CSADP created *The Diasporic Mind*, a quarterly webzine. *The Diasporic Mind* included the CSADP newsletter, academic essays, political opinions, and book, music, theater, and film reviews. The CSADP staff also formed the African Diaspora Research Coalition (ADRC), an academic work-group for UCLA graduate students. (The ADRC continues to meet and serves as a legacy of the CSADP).

The CSADP also cosponsored a screening of the award-winning film *PUNKS* and a discussion with the director/writer Patrik Ian-Polk. Cosponsors included the General Education Cluster in Interracial Dynamics and the Lesbian, Gay, Bisexual and Transgender Studies Program at UCLA.

In its final year, responsibility for the CSADP project was assumed by Darnell Hunt, the director of the UCLA Center for African American Studies. Under his leadership, the CSADP's final project has been to create this publication as a record of the efforts and achievements made by the dozens of people who have participated in the project over the years.

THIS VOLUME

What follows is an eclectic sampling of the studies, essays, reviews, and talks supported by the CSADP over its six-year life. While disparate in approach, style, and focus, these pieces all grapple, in one way or another, with the central problematic of tracing the connections between the material factors that continue to shape the lives of Africans in the diaspora and the world of ideas. In the end, these works unmask the "debate" over the relative importance of material factors versus ideas as largely diversionary: they are intricately connected. Culture is indeed the web of meaning that shapes both the world we see and the world we construct.

Accordingly, several themes are woven into the works in this volume:

—How social location shapes politics.

—How the global and local mutually determine one another.

—How the act of naming profoundly shapes what we think of our worlds and of ourselves.

—How pathological models of black culture deny the adaptive creativity of those who retain remnants of African culture.

—How states use representations of race to control marginalized populations.

—How marginalized populations use artistic production to resist state control.

The works in this volume survey not only the horrors, pain, and degradation associated with African experiences in the diaspora, but also the promise, adjustment, and innovation. To be sure, culture, the experiential linchpin, is sometimes revealed to be a double-edged sword.

Taken as whole, this volume demonstrates that the Cultural Studies in the African Diaspora Project was a dynamic and successful experiment in intellectual courage and innovation. It united scholars, students, cultural workers, communities, disciplines, and knowledge in an effort to document and explore new approaches to African Diaspora research. One of its greatest achievements was in paving the way for a whole new generation of scholars by inspiring and training the CSADP graduate student researchers who worked on the project over the years. By providing a greater context for a rich exchange of ideas, the CSADP contributed to contemporary discourse about African Diaspora peoples—celebrating their achievements, exploring their challenges, and imagining strategies for their survival and success in the new millennium.

THE THIRD WORLD RE-ORDER
LECTURE SERIES

IN HONOR OF CLAUDIA MITCHELL-KERNAN

This lecture series, presented during the 2001-2002 academic year, featured an interdisciplinary group of scholars who were invited to speak on a topic of their choice that addressed the question: "How can African Diaspora communities re-order the future?" Lectures addressed how twenty-first century members of African Diaspora communities can learn from their pasts, address current challenges, and prepare for impending struggles and victories. The lectures documented the contributions of African Diaspora communities to various world cultures and explored new ways of thinking and talking about the African Diaspora that will prepare peoples of African descent to recreate the meaning of race and identity in the new millennium. Speakers included: Kesha Fikes, John Jackson, Prudence Carter, Deborah Thomas, and Cynthia Young.

The series was presented in honor of Claudia Mitchell-Kernan in order to celebrate her extraordinary contributions to African Diaspora studies, as well as her support of the Cultural Studies in the African Diaspora Project. Claudia Mitchell-Kernan is Vice Chancellor and Dean of the Graduate Division, as well as a Professor of Anthropology and Psychiatry and Behavioral Sciences at UCLA. As a linguistic anthropologist, Dr. Mitchell-Kernan's ground-breaking research on the African American speech community has had a tremendous impact on the subsequent research of language in the African Diaspora. Her current work with Dr. M. Belinda Tucker on marriage in the African American community is poised to have a similar influence on future academic research on the subject. In addition to her work in these areas, Dr.

Mitchell-Kernan has also conducted widely respected research on the following subjects: children's discourse, Caribbean cultures, African American and Belizean youth culture, the impact of television on the socialization of children of color, and the challenges facing those who experience developmental delays.

Dr. Mitchell-Kernan served on the advisory board of the Cultural Studies in the African Diaspora Project from its inception, and has played an essential role in the project's enduring success. Dr. Mitchell-Kernan has consistently and passionately supported CSADP programming and CSADP graduate student researchers. For all of those involved in the project, Dr. Claudia Mitchell-Kernan has served as an advocate and an inspiration. This lecture series was presented in her honor because it was, indeed, an honor for all CSADP participants to work under her tutelage.

—D.B.

Synopsis of
ANGELA DAVIS AND THE U.S. THIRD WORLD LEFT

CYNTHIA YOUNG

This presentation is excerpted from a book project entitled *Soul Power: Culture, Radicalism and the U.S. Third World Left* that looks at how African Americans, Latino/as, and U.S. Asians conceptualized their cultural and political identities in relation to anticolonial movements in Africa, Asia, and the Caribbean. Focusing on the 1960s and 1970s, *Soul Power* follows a group of activists, artists, and writers who forged cultural, material, and ideological links to the Third World as a means of contesting economic, racial, and cultural hierarchies in the United States. *Soul Power*'s protagonists include LeRoi Jones (Amiri Baraka), Harold Cruse, Christine Choy, Susan Robeson, Charles Burnett, and Angela Y. Davis as well as groups such as Third World Newsreel and the Young Lords Party.

Central to this project is an assessment of the ways in which U.S. Third World Leftists' intellectual thought and political writing was influenced by relations between First World "minorities" and Third World "majorities." I am interested in how transnational political networks consolidated the routes through which peoples of color not only expressed international solidarity, but also gained insight into U.S.-based liberation struggles. A focus on Angela Yvonne Davis's early political activism and intellectual production has been enormously useful in helping me to explore these issues.

In the years since her high-profile trial on kidnapping, murder and conspiracy charges, Davis has become a Left icon, an aesthetic marker of the '60s, and a heroine to black youth nostalgic for a radical past they never knew.[1] The sensational facts of Davis's brush with the state and its police apparatus have become so well known that they are now relics of '60s lore. In 1970, Davis was placed on the FBI's "Ten Most Wanted" list in connection with a failed prison escape. When a national dragnet descended, she went underground until she was captured in New York City. Over the next two years, Davis became the most well known political prisoner in the nation as the struggle to "Free Angela Davis" sparked an international movement. Activists in Oakland, New York, Accra, and Havana signed petitions, raised money for her defense, and lobbied government officials. These events have since marked Davis as one of the central figures of the '60s, remaking her as a central figure in the Modern Civil Rights Movement.

Despite the assumption of Davis's centrality, she actually spent much of the decade, between 1960 and 1967, far removed from civil rights activism, living in the Northeast and traveling and studying in Paris and Frankfurt. In truth, her biography bears little resemblance to many civil rights activists. Unlike Ella Baker and Fannie Lou Hamer, for instance, she did not emerge from obscurity as a militant grassroots organizer of rural communities. Nor did she come to an understanding of international politics through an intense engagement with domestic racial politics as did figures such as Stokely Carmichael or Huey Newton. In fact, she followed the reverse trajectory. Davis's early internationalist orientation informed her anti-racist politics, rather than the other way around.

Placing Davis within a larger anticolonial context complicates our understanding of her work and the U.S. liberation struggles in which she participated. Resituating Davis within the U.S. Third World Left, I seek to understand how her early sense of anticolonial solidarity and transnational identification shaped her approach to race and class oppression. A "revolutionary internationalism" profoundly informed her political and intellectual development. That internationalism combined elements of Marxism, feminism, and anticolonialism into a political analysis characterized by a focus on state violence and incarceration as First World techniques for maintaining racial oppression. In exploring Davis's early work, I highlight the impact that Western Marxists and Third World anticolonialists had on Davis's praxis and theory, and then examine its articulation in the essay, "Political Prisoners, Prisons, and Black Liberation." In doing so, I demonstrate the ways in which an international anticolonial front facilitated radical anti-racist activism in the U.S.

Born in Birmingham, Alabama, Davis's early life was indelibly shaped by the routine indignities of Jim Crow segregation, economic discrimination, and brutal terrorism. Though Davis's family was relatively privileged within Birmingham's black community, her parents were politically active. They were both members of the local NAACP chapter, and her mother was also a national officer in the Southern Negro Youth Congress, a Communist Party USA (CPUSA)-affiliated organization (James 1998). The adolescent Davis, however, was not politically active, spending much of her time at the public library seeking what she describes in her autobiography as an "avenue of escape" (Davis 1974). She found one in 1959 when she won a Quaker scholarship that landed her at a progressive high school in Greenwich Village.

It was at the radical Elizabeth Irwin/Little Red School House, a haven for blacklisted schoolteachers, that the young Davis first encountered Marxist theory. In her history classes she read Marx and Engels' *Communist Manifesto*, supplementing it with lectures by radical historian Herbert Aptheker at the American Institute for Marxist Studies. Davis also joined Advance, a CPUSA-affiliated youth organization to which Bettina Aptheker, Eugene Davis, and Mary Lou Patterson, daughter of black Communist attorney William Patterson, also belonged.

After graduation in 1961, Davis matriculated at Brandeis University in Massachusetts. While there, Davis studied with James Baldwin and met Herbert Marcuse, the Frankfurt School philosopher and media-anointed "New Left theorist" with whom she developed a lasting personal and intellectual relationship. During her college years, Davis's intensive study of French, German, and the Western philosophical tradition was refracted through the harrowing news reports of the civil rights movement and her encounters with anticolonial activists, particularly those from Algeria, Vietnam, and Cuba.

In 1962, Davis visited Paris on her way to the *Eighth World Festival for Youth* in Helsinki, Finland. While there, she witnessed firsthand the racist attacks against Algerians, reflecting, "[t]o be an Algerian living in Paris in 1962 was to be a hunted human being" (Davis 1974). Comparing the situation of Algerians and black Americans, Davis concluded that the French police "were as vicious as the red-neck cops in Birmingham who met the Freedom Riders with their dogs and hoses....The new places, the new experiences I had expected to discover through travel turned out to be the same old places, the same old experiences with a common message of struggle" (Davis 1974). In Paris, Davis was also confronted with the intense culture of resistance forged by Vietnamese immigrants living in Paris, an experience that sparked her thinking about the U.S. as an imperial nation. However, it was the example set by the Cuban Revolution that most profoundly influenced Davis's future direction.[2] In her autobiography, Davis recalls that it was the young Cuban militants (many of them women) whom she met at the Helsinki Conference that conveyed "a fiercely compelling spirit of revolution," satirizing the way "wealthy American capitalists had invaded their country and robbed them of all traces of sovereignty." Davis's interest in Cuba culminated in a month-long trip in July 1969, which she characterizes in her autobiography as "a great climax in my life" that left a "permanent mark on my existence" (Davis 1974).

For Davis, the domestic civil rights movement was beginning to fit into an anticolonial framework in which Third World peoples and African Americans might find a common basis for struggle. During her senior year, Davis sought Marcuse's advice on a course of philosophical study, a meeting that led to weekly one-on-one tutoring sessions with the philosopher himself. It was those sessions that prompted Davis's decision to study German idealism and Enlightenment philosophy with Theodor Adorno in Frankfurt, Germany.

Though she wrote a thesis under Adorno's direction by the summer of 1967, Davis was anxious to return to the U.S. where racial struggle was simmering. Relocating to Los Angeles, California, she began working on a Ph.D. with Marcuse at UC San Diego while becoming increasingly active in radical politics. She joined the CPUSA and began doing political organizing on behalf of black political prisoners, speaking and writing in defense of the Soledad Brothers who had been accused of killing a white prison guard. One of the defendants was George Jackson who had been sentenced at the age of 17 to one year to life in prison for a $70 gas station hold-up. While in prison, Jackson became a member of the Black Panther Party and a student of Marxism-Leninism, teaching himself Western and Third World philosophy and politics. It was Davis's efforts on behalf of Jackson that eventually led to her arrest.

Thus it is in the context of Third World anticolonialism and intensive Marxist study that Davis's later political activism must be seen; in fact, she emerged from a very particular anticolonial moment. Increasingly, radicals in the U.S. and elsewhere recognized and targeted the U.S. as a producer and disseminator of a new imperialism premised on the fiction of free markets, and the triumph of (state protected) capitalism.[3] If Davis's commitment to Marxism, feminism, anticolonialism, and anti-racism shaped her political activism, it also directly impacted her intellectual output. In "Political Prisoners, Prison and Black Liberation," she uses an intersectional approach to critique both U.S. state policies and radical movements against the state.

In "Political Prisoners, Prison and Black Liberation," Davis focuses on the political uses of incarceration, aiming to unsettle the system of laws and the practices of criminalization that maintain social inequality and fortify a repressive U.S. state. Since enslavement, she argues, black people have been repeatedly "compelled to openly violate those laws which directly or indirectly buttress our oppression." Defending the person who breaks the law "in the interests of a class or a people," Davis describes the ways in which the U.S. state has rendered the very category of "political prisoner" null and void. Citing the cases of International Workers of the World (IWW) organizer Joe Hill and armed self-defense advocate Robert Williams, Davis concludes, "The offense of the political prisoner is political boldness, the persistent challenging—legally or extra-legally—of fundamental social wrongs fostered and reinforced by the state" (James 1998).

The essay takes a more interesting turn when Davis returns to the figure of the "self-interested" criminal. Asserting that "the majority of criminal offenses bear a direct relationship to property" Davis argues that the prison functions as an "instrument of class domination" (James 1998). Comparing the black and brown U.S. prisoner to her anticolonial counterpart, she asserts that ghetto police are akin to Algerian colonial forces. The description of all prisoners as "political prisoners" hinges upon Davis's view of black, Chicano, and Puerto Rican communities as "nationally oppressed." Ghettos are geographically isolated and economically exploited areas where a black and brown reserve labor army is warehoused.[4]

At this point, Davis then pushes the Marxian framework upon which she has thus far depended, challenging (and here she acknowledges her debt to the Black Panther Party) the traditional Marxist dismissal of the "criminal class" as part of a lumpen proletariat that is inherently untrustworthy and unimportant to the "coming" revolution. Building a systematic case, Davis not only stretches the framework of class analysis, but demonstrates that Marxists ignore race at their political and ideological peril. In fact, she argues, the deconstruction and destruction of U.S. imperialism depends upon crafting theory that connects state violence, incarceration, racist repression, and colonialism.

In her early work, Davis drew upon Marxist theory and anticolonial encounters in order to produce an analysis that connected the plight of First World minorities and Third World majorities. Looking at the ways in which state domination, colonialism, and Western imperialism intersect, she investigated the ways in which racism and colonialism structure new racialized hierarchies with global impact. Placing Third World anticolonialism and First World anti-racist struggles in productive tension enabled Davis to radically critique the political, economic, and social workings of the U.S. nation-state. Examining the political and intellectual legacy of Angela Davis enables a reconsideration of the role of black radicalism and transnational identification in dismembering the body of U.S. imperialism.

ENDNOTES

[1] For Davis's own take on the fetishizing of her image from the '60s, see Angela Y. Davis, "Afro Images: Politics, Fashion and Nostalgia." In *The Angela Y. Davis Reader,* edited by Joy James (Malden, MA: Blackwell Publishers Inc., 1998).

[2] Davis was not alone in being influenced by the Cuban Revolution. See my article "Havana Up in Harlem: LeRoi Jones, Harold Cruse and the Making of a Cultural Revolution," *Science and Society,* Winter 2001: 12-38.

[3] During the period, the internal colony thesis enjoyed renewed popularity with radicals of color. For other articulations of this thesis in contemporaneous texts, see Nelson Peery, *The Negro National Colonial Question,* 2nd Revised Edition (Chicago: Workers Press, 1975); Harold Cruse, *The Crisis of the Negro Intellectual* (New York: Morrow, 1967); Robert Allen, *Black Awakening in Capitalist America,* 1st Edition (Garden City, N.Y.: Doubleday, 1969); or Mario Barerra, Carlos Munoz, and Charles Ornelas, "The Barrio as Internal Colony." In *La Causa Politica: A Chicano Politics Reader*, edited by F. Chris Garcia (Notre Dame: University of Notre Dame Press, 1972).

[4] For this particular articulation, I am indebted to Nikhil Singh, "The Black Panthers and the 'Undeveloped Country' of the Left." In *The Black Panther Party Reconsidered,* edited by Charles E. Jones, 57-105. (Baltimore: Black Classic Press, 1998).

BIBLIOGRAPHY

Allen, Robert. *Black Awakening in Capitalist America* 1st Edition. Garden City, N.Y.: Doubleday, 1969.

Barerra, Mario, Carlos Munoz and Charles Ornelas. "The Barrio as Internal Colony" In *La Causa Politica: A Chicano Politics Reader,* edited by F. Chris Garcia. Notre Dame: University of Notre Dame Press, 1972.

Cruse, Harold. *The Crisis of the Negro Intellectual.* New York: Morrow, 1969.

Davis, Angela Y. *With My Mind on Freedom: An Autobiography.* New York: Random House, Inc., 1974.

James, Joy. *The Angela Y. Davis Reader.* Malden, M.A.: Blackwell Publishers, 1998.

Peery, Nelson. *The Negro National Colonial Question,* 2nd Revised Edition. Chicago: Workers Press, 1975.

Singh, Nikhil. "The Black Panthers and the 'Undeveloped Country' of the Left". In *The Black Panther Party Reconsidered,* edited by Charles E. Jones, 57-105. Baltimore: Black Classic Press, 1998.

Young, Cynthia. "Havana Up in Harlem," *Science and Society,* Winter 2001: 12-38.

RADICALLY CAPITALIST GHETTO FEMINISTS: THE POLITICS OF RACE, CLASS, AND GENDER IN CONTEMPORARY JAMAICA

DEBORAH A. THOMAS

As dancehall—and youth popular culture more generally—has become the reference point against which Jamaicans of all social classes define themselves, there has been significant academic and popular debate regarding the ways women are portrayed through, and participate in, dancehall culture. The central issue within these debates has been that of "respectability" (or the purported lack thereof), itself a recurring trope within the social scientific literature on the Caribbean. Within Jamaica, the preoccupation with respectability has reflected a nationalist nervousness. By this I mean that the post-emancipation imposition of Victorian gender ideologies intended to relegate women to the private sphere spilled over to the nationalist period of the mid-twentieth century and was reflected through the concern with family structure and its relationship to economic productivity and national unity. In this way, the concern with privatizing women (and developing respectability within the private sphere) was really a concern with state formation (and developing respectability in an international public sphere that by the end of World War II held the nation up as the most sovereign and modern form of social organization). This concern has been ongoing and has been expressed in various ways since Jamaica's independence in 1962. The public spectre of the marginally-clad, loud-mouthed, and ultimately "disrespectful" dancehall woman, therefore, has provoked a considerable degree of consternation and anxiety.

I will be exploring the implications of what I call "ghetto feminism"—a feminist praxis espoused through popular cultural forms that are associated with lower-class black Jamaicans. This is a praxis that publicly challenges both middle-class notions of respectability and progress, and men's notions of submissive female availability. "Ghetto feminism" is also part of a broader cultural complex I have defined as "modern blackness"—an ethos that embodies the late-twentieth century public shift away from the creole multi-racialism that was consolidated during the mid-twentieth century nationalist movement.[1] This shift is critical to understanding the politics of race, class, and gender in contemporary Jamaica. It is a shift that has been due, in part, to contemporary processes of globalization, and in particular, the intensification of transnational migration and the proliferation of media technologies. One of the results of this shift is that the influence of that sector of the professional middle-classes who gained state power at independence, and who have served as cultural and political brokers in the lives of poorer Jamaicans, has diminished. As a result, while black Jamaicans negotiate recent transformations in global capitalist development in order to chart new possibilities for their lives, they are changing both the content of publicly espoused visions of progress, and the media through which these visions are expressed.

What is especially significant here is that as black lower-class Jamaicans—and particularly women—have attempted to expand the scope of their economic resources, they have not necessarily simultaneously endeavored to emulate the standards of respectability and sociocultural capital that have been associated with the professional and clerical middle classes and that were, to some extent, institutionalized by the nationalist state. Rather, they have developed a racialized working-class expression of the dominant elite ethos of global capitalism, even as they have simultaneously exposed, critiqued, and satirized that ethos. As a result, modern blackness is urban, migratory, based in youth-oriented popular culture, and influenced by African American popular style. It is individualistic, radically capitalist, and, as I have noted, "ghetto feminist." Because modern blackness is expressed through the idioms and cultural leadership of lower-class black Jamaicans, it has reversed the status quo and called into question the legitimacy of Jamaican middle- and upper-classes' cultural and political leadership.

My exploration of ghetto feminism and modern blackness will take two tacks. First, I'll lay out a theoretical discussion that more fully defines ghetto feminism as a public ideology within the national public sphere. Second, I'll use the themes raised within a local theatrical production to speak in more grounded terms about how individuals at the local level negotiate these newly public ideologies, and relate them to their own lives and experiences. These discussions are framed within a couple of arguments that I should clarify here. First, we need to understand people's choices—especially those that sometimes seem contradictory—within a framework that takes into account both their locally specific histories, and the ways they have been affected by processes of globalization, themselves two-sided. Secondly, we must maintain a nuanced analysis that clarifies the ways people manipulate and take advantage of the changing structures of opportunity surrounding them—sometimes transforming and sometimes reproducing relations of power and inequality—rather than one that positions people either as duped, or as powerless to resist, reinvent, or renovate.

GHETTO FEMINISM: "Yuh Nuh Ready Fi Dis Yet, Bwoy"[2]

While modern blackness is not reducible to dancehall culture, it is also inseparable from it. Dancehall music and its associated culture became increasingly popular in the mid-1980s and especially after the death of Bob Marley. Where previous reggae music had emphasized social critique and a belief in redemption, early dancehall music reflected a ghetto glorification of sex, guns, and the drug trade. This has led many observers to refer to dancehall derisively as "slackness" music, vulgarly degrading to Jamaica's moral fiber. For example, one newspaper report declared that dancehall's rhythm "produces violent reactions in the body," and that its lyrics—"statements of raw protest, dismissal, incitements to violence, unbridled anger, and crude explicit sexuality"—were a root cause of the negativism and aggressive selfishness that permeated the society (Whylie 1997). Similarly, a letter to the editor in the *Jamaica Gleaner* contended that dancehall "promotes and glorifies a certain moral incorrectness and feeds the people a distorted view of life" (Chance 1997). These arguments, framed in terms of morality, also speak to an ongoing concern, a fear even, among the middle classes regarding the relative power of popular culture to shape both behavior and public perceptions of Jamaica and Jamaicans.

The diatribe against dancehall, however, has not merely been moored in morality. Dancehall's distancing from the revolutionary politics of the 1970s, and its reflection of the personal melodramas of making it in the marketplace, have led some to characterize it as politically conservative. This critique is associated not only with the left-leaning Jamaican intelligentsia, but also with sectors of poorer Jamaicans, including prominent Rastafarians. These critics have viewed dancehall as denigrating to black people, and especially women, and therefore as serving the ruling elements in society. While several organizations have taken a public stance against the explicit misogyny and homophobia that characterize some dancehall lyrics, some scholars have viewed the cultural space of dancehall as facilitating a form of female liberation. Carolyn Cooper, a Jamaican literary critic, has argued that dancehall is a kind of "verbal marronage" (Cooper 1989,12) through which singers critique the conservatism of Jamaican social relations. Similarly, ethnomusicologist Ken Bilby's view is that dancehall discourse simply rehearses ideologies espoused more generally within Jamaican society (1995). What these kinds of assessments flag is the need to analyze dancehall within an historical framework that links popular cultural representations of gender and sexuality to the continuities and changes within more general societal norms.

Peggy Antrobus has remarked that while she was working as the first director of the Jamaican government's Women's Bureau during the mid-1970s, she discovered that black lower-class women defined their two primary sources of power as sexuality—but not necessarily sex, and spirituality—but not necessarily religion. By highlighting the centrality of sexuality to women's power, she draws attention to what I have identified as "ghetto feminism." Here, I am arguing that the concern with "slackness" in dancehall has not only been related to the glorification of materialism, violence, and sexual explicitness, but also to the public emergence of ghetto feminism, most clearly embodied through the persona of the scantily-clad and sexually-explicit female DJ. The public emergence of this persona within popular culture has been critical precisely because her gender politics challenge two primary aspects of the creole nationalist project—the pursuit of respectability and the acceptance of a paternalistic patriarchy.[3]

The trope of respectability has its roots in Jamaica's post-emancipation period. The Baptist Church played a major role in post-emancipation rural settlement by buying and subdividing properties in order to establish church communities called "free villages." Within these villages, former slaves aspiring to be Christian blacks could take advantage of the missionary churches and schools in order to establish new claims to status, to acquire new skills, and to question "why Christian values were not practiced in the society they knew" (Turner 1982, 94). At the same time, the Baptist missionaries mobilized new gender ideologies to support their view of restructured economic, political, and social life after emancipation. Historian Catherine Hall has demonstrated that the Baptists viewed slavery as having produced a situation in which male slaves, dependent on their masters, were unable to become "real men." That is, they were unable to live up to the standards of middle class Englishmen at the time—understood as "being married, being independent in 'pecuniary affairs,' working for wages, being a householder, paying for medical care and education, celebrating the voluntary principle which was at the heart of dissenting politics, [and] refusing state intervention in church, school and welfare" (1995, 53). For the Baptists, emancipation marked the potential for the former slaves to become "white"—but not like the white men and women of plantation society. Rather, black men would become "responsible, independent, industrious, domesticated Christians" and black women, now focused on marriage and child-rearing, would "no longer be sexually subjugated to their masters but properly dependent on their husbands" (1995, 54).[4] However, this potential was dependent upon erasing the social and religious ideologies held by the population during slavery, ideologies the missionaries understood as being African in derivation. These missionaries' fatal flaw, then, rested upon their refusal to recognize an existing black culture and their related inability to apprehend the fact that marriage failed to become popular, that the birth of children outside of wedlock remained the norm, and that women's labor and land tenure continued to be of utmost importance to the communities they were serving. Nevertheless, the rhetoric of respectability survived the decline of the missionary communities.

By the mid-twentieth century, the British imperial state and the local nationalist elite both envisioned a particular ideological and material structure within which men and women would create respectable families and contribute to community and national life. The emphasis on the creation of nuclear family households within the "Report of the West Indian Royal Commission" after the 1938 labor rebellions, reflected the dominance of the Parsonian integrationist framework within research and policy circles at the time. This framework upheld a view of the family as the determining institution of sociopolitical and economic stability, but this was a family in which males were central as breadwinners so that women could be primarily concerned with social reproduction in the private sphere. Again, this arrangement has never been hegemonic (nor, even, necessarily desired) within the British West Indies. Throughout the English-speaking Caribbean, women's economic production has been central not only to the constitution of West Indian families, but also to their own independent cultivation and maintenance of social networks and kin ties.[5] Nevertheless, the cultivation of "respectability" has remained both a key issue within popular debate and an important tool within academic analysis.

Various changes in Jamaica's political economy and gendered division of labor since independence have altered the structural dimensions of women's public lives. The establishment of the first Women's Bureau within the Caribbean by Michael Manley's government in 1973 brought women's development issues to the fore at the same time that the government began to massively recruit female labor in order to reduce national unemployment levels. Throughout the 1980s, national development strategies continued to target female labor on an unprecedented scale, as priority plans for economic development were based on the expansion of free-trade zones, offshore data processing, and tourism (Ford-Smith 1997). Meanwhile, the implementation of IMF-induced structural adjustment policies, the fantastic expansion of the informal sector in which women figure prominently as "higglers," and the growth of an internationally-mobile female labor force have ensured that women remain within the public sphere, both as laborers, and as service-providers for their families. While these shifts have not occasioned a full-scale overhaul of the structural and ideological bases of gender inequality and hierarchy in Jamaica, they have enabled some women to begin to redefine their public image in their own terms, often within the space of dancehall. These are women who have eschewed attempts to cultivate the social standards of femininity and respectability associated with middle- and upper-class Jamaicans because they no longer view the consequences of failing to assimilate as critical with respect to their economic survival (Ulysse 1999; cf. Ford-Smith 1997). At the same time, middle- and upper-class Jamaicans have been forced to acknowledge their power, as Gina Ulysse has argued, "if for no other reason than because they now also possess and manipulate the hegemonic U.S. dollar" (1999, 168).[6]

Ghetto feminism not only publicly challenges the rhetoric of respectability, but also issues a critique of patriarchy, principally through its public affirmation of female sexual desire. This critique is most evident in the work of female dancehall DJs such as Tanya Stephens and Lady Saw. For example, Tanya Stephens encourages women to chastise men for satisfying themselves but leaving them "hot like a ginger,"[7] and tells men that the consequences of such behavior are that women will find their satisfaction elsewhere:

> Have yuh ever stop to think wha mek a gal cheat
> Yuh need fi check yuhself before yuh start kiss yuh teeth
> Caw yuh nuh ready fi this yet bwoy
> Have yuh ever wonder what mek a girl cum
> A woman fus fi satisfy before yuh say yuh done
> Yuh caan say a thing if yuh end up a get bun
> Caw yuh nuh ready fi this yet bwoy
>
> Tanya Stephens, lyrics from "Yuh Nuh Ready"

Similarly, Lady Saw enjoins women to take material advantage of the power embodied within the commodity they control—access to sexual favors:

> Mi have mi light bill fi pay man haffi mind mi
> Man haffi buy mi everyting before dem wine mi
> Mi have rent fi deal with all tomorrow morning'
> So no likkle fool caan strip mi
> Me waan go a Bahamas for Sunday
> An come back to mi husband Monday
> But 'tis a fool mi a look fi nyam out him bank book
> If dem know what me know dem jus 'low mi
>
> Lady Saw, lyrics from "Man Haffi Mind Wi"

What this kind of discourse publicly counters is an unchecked male dominance, a dominance that is related to particular ideologies about Jamaican masculinity that emerged within the context of plantation slavery and that have continued without significant modification through the contemporary period.[8] Anthropologist Lisa Douglass has argued that these ideologies are generalized throughout the male population— that is, "what makes a man a man is this prerogative to receive the services and request the attention of a woman" (Douglass 1992, 251). She contrasts this to the ways ideologies about femininity constitute class-specific attitudes and behaviors that are linked to color and are valued differently by the society as a whole (1992). Within this context, a woman's decision to make the level of her attention contingent upon the extent to which a man can provide her with what she needs or wants materially destabilizes this paradigm, as it presents a threat not only to that individual man's masculinity, but also to the patriarchal ideological framework that positions this masculinity as transcendently powerful. Worse yet, is the negation of this power that occurs when a woman publicly insults a man's sexual ability. The ghetto feminism proclaimed by a Tanya Stephens or a Lady

Saw, therefore, eschews the model of privatized female sexuality associated with middle-class femininity and respectability. I am not suggesting here that Jamaican women have only recently begun to use these tactics to carve out spaces for their own power vis-à-vis the men within their intimate social worlds. What I am noting, however, is that dancehall has created a space for a new public advocacy of these tactics by black lower-class women for black lower-class women. Further, this is a space that exists beyond the realm of intimate relations and as such, it has the potential to infiltrate a more general political vision.

The obvious contemporary parallel to the ghetto feminism of modern blackness in the United States is hip-hop. As has been the case with dancehall, several scholars have argued that while hip-hop can present images of women that are offensive, it also allows women "a way to defy traditional gender roles, assert independence, and demand respect" and "provides a forum for feminist action" (Grappo 2001, 27; cf. Rose 1994; Morgan 1999).[9] For these scholars, irreverent and sexually-explicit rappers like Foxy Brown and Lil' Kim are not merely pawns of a sexist recording industry—indeed, a sexist culture—that can't get enough of brown-skinned T&A. Instead, they are independent, they demand respect, and they refuse to discount women's sexual desires and pleasures. That is, they are part of a more general struggle over control of black female sexuality.

I am aware that locating women's attempts to redefine their own sexual imagery as a feminist practice is controversial, especially if these redefinitions seem to reproduce some dominant tropes about black women even as it challenges others. Indeed, black feminists in the U.S. have been wary of condoning the use of erotic power as a means of battling sexism, expressly because of the historical legacies enfolding black female sexuality. Moreover, as journalist Joan Morgan has pointed out, "[w]ithout financial independence, education, ambition, intelligence, spirituality, and love, punanny alone isn't all that powerful. The reality is that it's easily replaceable, inexhaustible in supply, and quite frankly, common" (1999, 224). At the same time, hip-hop feminists and dancehall divas push the envelope, generate public debate, and broaden what is possible in terms of public behavior for women. The extensive public controversy about the representations of women and female sexuality that surround such artistes as Lady Saw and Tanya Stephens, therefore, has to do with the perceived threat they issue to middle class morality, to lower-class visions of black female integrity and respectability, to many Caribbean feminists' vision of transformation, to male supremacy, and to the project of state formation itself.

It is also the case that while many women appreciate aspects of these DJs' politics, very few emulate their self-presentation in a daily fashion. Instead, their attraction to Tanya Stephens or Lady Saw is more akin to living vicariously through the images they present. This brings us to a discussion of more locally rendered representations of the intersections of gender, race, class in late-twentieth century Jamaica. Here, I will present one example—a Roots play written by a woman named Winsome, a black lower-class Jamaican in her mid-thirties who grew up in the community where I conducted my field research. I use this example in order to provide some insight into how representations and ideologies circulating within the national public sphere are appropriated, debated, and modified within public fora at the local level.

Roots Plays

Roots plays are part of the culture that has developed around dancehall music.[10] These popular plays, performed in patois, draw from a variety of stock characters to humorously present situations familiar to their largely lower-class audiences. They intersperse popular dancehall songs throughout, in order to push the action along, or to underline a particular theme. Middle-class theatre-goers often denigrate these plays as "trashy." That is, they do not consider Roots plays to be real art and argue that they do not reflect appropriate values or desirable lifestyles. Nevertheless, successful Roots plays can be very lucrative for their producers, promoters, and performers, and they provide a space where these alternative values and lifestyles are both vindicated and debated by lower-class audiences. Winsome wrote and produced her own Roots plays as a means of expressing her vision of Jamaican life, and of earning additional money to supplement her income as the accounts keeper for a public institution. Thematically, Winsome's plays explored the intersections of sex, money, and power in human relationships—themes she felt were relevant to the day-to-day experiences of the majority of the population. In 1997, she was working on a play entitled "Ruff Rider," which was ultimately performed in three venues outside of Kingston. "Ruff Rider" is the story of the making and unmaking of a household that includes Monica, her husband Earl, their son Skim Milk—so named for his penchant for ingesting the family's supply of milk powder—and their niece Bella. The story, ultimately, is a morality tale about the consequences of sexual betrayal and dishonesty.

"Ruff Rider"

The play begins by establishing the characters of Monica as the hard-working, long-suffering wife; Earl as the ever-philandering (and therefore fast-talking) husband; and Skim Milk as the fun-loving, yet mercenary, son. When Skim Milk discovers his father attempting to have sex with Bella while she is sleeping, he extorts money from both of them —first from Earl, who insists he keep his mouth shut, and second from Bella, who entreats him to tell his mother the truth. When the moment of reckoning arrives, Skim Milk betrays his promise to Bella, and Monica threatens to throw Bella out of the house for attempting to seduce her husband. Bella pleads with Earl, saying she'll do anything for him if he can convince Monica to let her stay in the household. Earl grabs his crotch and asks "anything … including this?" and Bella agrees.

Later, we are introduced to Sarah Bunjaws, recently arrived from the country to work as the family's new (and not-so-bright) household helper. Sarah, too, becomes the object of Earl's advances, but is ultimately protected by Bella, who reluctantly agrees to let Sarah tag along to her job. Bella works in a club as a go-go dancer alongside Mystic, a dancehall deejay upon whom she has a crush. At the club, much to Bella's chagrin, Sarah and Mystic become smitten with each other. Bella, therefore, resolves to remove her competition, both from the house and from Mystic's life. She discovers a love letter that Sarah had written to Mystic and deviously changes Mystic's name, addressing it instead to Earl and leaving it where Monica will see it. Indeed, Monica finds the letter and throws Sarah out of the house. Bella then goes to visit Mystic who refuses her advances, arguing that he could never forgive Bella for the devious way she got Sarah kicked out of the house.

Meanwhile, Earl returns unexpectedly from a temporary labor gig "in foreign" and wants to sneak "a stab" from Bella before Monica knows he's back in Jamaica. As they moan and groan in the bedroom, Monica arrives home early from work and discovers them. She runs after both of them as Bella pleads, "Auntie, me tell yuh but you never waan believe me and me haffi do this to stay ina the house." The scene ends with Monica pummeling Earl with a piece of board. The last scene takes place in the club where, thanks to Skim Milk's encouragement, Sarah and Mystic have reconciled. Monica enters on the arm of a tall, dark, and handsome stranger. Eventually, Earl also arrives and begs for Monica's forgiveness. Monica, however, tells him that on top of everything else, he can't even satisfy her in bed, and so she has found another man. The play ends with the commotion that ensues when Earl picks up a cutlass to threaten Monica's new man.

In "Ruff Rider," Winsome presents us with a world where the more lucrative economic opportunities are generated either by migrating or by working within the popular culture industry. She also allows us to see the ways in which both of these dimensions are gendered. That is, the young rural woman comes to the city and finds work as a household helper, but the "man of the house" seeks labor contracts abroad; the young urban woman finds a job as a go-go dancer, but the male youth tries his luck DJing. Monica's work, on the other hand, remains unspecified, providing the most consistent income for the household but apparently without any glitz or glamour. "Ruff Rider" also explores ideologies about appropriate female behavior. For example, Bella's lifestyle is portrayed as exciting, but also unfulfilling. Sarah Bunjaws is depicted as slow and unsophisticated, but the "good country girl" ultimately gets her man. Though Winsome renders an intense distrust between women and men, she also leaves us with the idea that "true love" triumphs over adversity and repels pretenders, who are ultimately left to fend for themselves in the sexual marketplace. In this way, "Ruff Rider" ultimately seems to recuperate the respectability narrative. At the same time, it also challenges the unquestioned acceptance of male dominance through Monica's ultimate rejection of Earl at the end of the play. Indeed, her final insult—that Earl couldn't satisfy her sexually—resolves the issue of male infidelity not through an appeal to some abstracted sense of morality but by publicly advertising consequences and validating female sexual desire and pleasure. The "happy ending" of "Ruff Rider," then, rests on everybody getting what they deserve. Sarah and Mystic find true love with the encouragement of Skim Milk, Bella and her aunt reconcile, Earl is left frustrated, and Monica can finally balance her hard work with some love and pleasure of her own.

Winsome has written other plays—as well as a children's novel —that also address similar themes and issues. In all of her work, the sympathetic characters are those she portrays as struggling to balance their own pursuit of individual gain with "living well together" with others. As they negotiate the fine line between egalitarianism and hierarchy, her characters also contribute to the public debate regarding the gendered dimensions of respectability and reputation. It is not only the characters or the narrative that make Roots plays especially significant embodiments of modern blackness (internal dialogues), but also aspects of their performances.

Rehearsing (and Producing) Roots

The rehearsal and production processes for Roots plays are substantially different from those of nationally established performance companies. For the production of "Ruff Rider," Winsome rehearsed her actors at public parks in Kingston, and during rehearsals, most of the time was focused on making sure people knew the script. There was some attention to directing the manner in which specific lines were delivered or in blocking particular actions, but most of this was left up to the actor. In Winsome's case, rehearsal time was a luxury, so a "good actor," in her view, was one who could fend for him or herself, and one who could develop his or her own appropriate "body language" without extensive direction. Consequently, each actor needed to be familiar enough with what they were portraying to be convincingly funny and human. Additionally, because there was little time for an extended rehearsal process, and because the group couldn't enter the performance space prior to the day of the show, the actors rarely rehearsed "full out," that is, they seldom practiced the play straight through at performance level. This meant that even Winsome was never quite sure what she would ultimately get from actors with whom she had not previously worked.

To produce her plays, Winsome made all the arrangements with the venues and handled all the publicity herself. She tried to pay the actors per performance, and to reimburse them for transportation and one meal. Occasionally, but not often, she was able to obtain sponsorship for a portion of her expenses, and one or two of the middle-class members of her community helped her from time to time. She complained that her children's father didn't really support her involvement in theater, and that he had become jealous of the time it took her away from him, time spent developing close relationships with others. With one or two exceptions, he hadn't attended her productions, and as a result, she felt that he didn't "stand up beside me like a man." She argued that this had also caused her financial problems from time to time. One of her more successful plays, for example, didn't make as much money as Winsome had expected because at every venue where it was performed, someone stole either the bar or the admission money, which at one location was approximately U.S. $1,700. In her estimation, this wouldn't have happened had her children's father been there keeping an eye on the cash box. Still, she maintained that she wouldn't give up her theater for anyone because it was what she could do to express herself, something just for her.

Winsome found it difficult to produce her plays in Kingston. This was, in part, because the cost of renting theatres in the city was prohibitive, and because the theatres, usually booked months in advance, didn't generally rent their space on a per night basis. Additionally, some of the managers of the more popular theatre venues in Kingston were hesitant to produce Roots plays because, as they argued, the plays were "too loud" and "too focused on sex." Winsome dismissed this argument, suggesting that Roots plays were no louder than U.S. movies, and were far less sexually explicit. In her estimation, "uptown" theatres in Kingston discriminated against Roots plays because they did not want to portray the lives of the "poorer class of people." As a result, she noted that she usually had more luck in rural areas.

To produce "Ruff Rider" in one venue, Winsome made arrangements with the director of a local community center and youth association, and agreed upon a total fee of about U.S. $150, half of which would go to the owner of a local sound system who would provide the music. When these arrangements were settled, the actors, in conjunction with supportive family members, were involved in advertising the play, supplying costumes, and building the set. When the actors were ready to begin the performance, the selector stopped the music that he had been playing and announced that it was "showtime," and so they started. Throughout the play, there was substantial involvement on the part of the audience who, far from being passive spectators, commented on the action and interacted with the characters. For example, they enthusiastically encouraged Uncle Earl in his sexual advances toward both Bella and Sarah, and especially when he returned unexpectedly from "foreign" to "get a stab" from Bella, by shouting "yu cyaan come from foreign and get no pussy!" However, they objected to Skim Milk's attempts at the same, arguing that he should get out of his father's way. They also condemned Bella's efforts to come between Mystic and Sarah, yelling out "lef' it man" when she discovered Sarah's love letter and "you cyaan get him back" when she went to Mystic's house. Audience members also let the cast know when they couldn't hear ("use the microphone!"), and cued the individuals in charge of the lights and music ("play selector!"). The actors also interacted directly with the audience. For example, the character Earl shushed the audience when he was trying to trick Bella into having sex with him while she was asleep, and when the audience said they couldn't hear, the actors on stage moved closer to a microphone and passed it back and forth between them to deliver their lines. Additionally, about two-thirds of the way through the performance when someone backstage received word that several people were still arriving, the actor who was playing Earl asked the audience whether they would mind if they started the play again from the beginning since so many people were just coming. The audience agreed, and so the actors took it from the top.

This kind of dialogic and participatory relationship between the performers and audience members has long been seen as characteristic of black vernacular cultures throughout the Atlantic world. It is a relationship that does not demarcate the performer from his or her community, and also one that encourages real-time reinterpretation, admiration, and critique. The lack of separation between performer/ performance and audience/performance is further marked through the production process. For example, Winsome's play started without the kinds of signals common within theatrical venues associated with middle-class theatre-goers, like a blackout. Moreover, by addressing the audience directly and starting the play over, the actors broke the "fourth wall," that symbolic boundary that typically separates performers from spectators. Of course, this "wall" was also broken when audience members shouted directions and commentary to characters and technical staff. The rural outdoor setting facilitated this kind of interaction, which, though characteristic of Roots plays more generally, was more boisterous than is the tendency in indoor venues. Finally, the structure of Roots plays, and the nature of the relationship between the audience and the performers, allows for a degree of improvisation within the script. This improvisation might be spurred by a comment made by a particular audience member, or by other concurrent events. For example, during the intermission for a play performed in a rural Manchester Parish, someone from the community was shot in the town square. When the play resumed, the actor who played the character of the strong, tough mother figure chastised the "bad boy" character, asking "was yu kill de man ina de square?!" The "bad boy" character denied the accusation, and after a bit of improvisation about what had just happened outside the theatre, the actors resumed their written lines. Though many Roots plays are performed in theatres in Kingston, low-budget and community-oriented performances like Winsome's neither approximated nor sought to emulate the production standards associated with more established theatrical venues. Instead, cast and audience members worked together with what was common to their community to generate an alternative institutional framework for their own creative expressions.

CONCLUSION

The themes raised within Winsome's plays and the processes by which they are performed open a window for us to nuance our understanding of "modern blackness," and in particular my earlier discussion about "ghetto feminism." Here, I want to highlight two discrete, though intimately related, points. First, I mean to stress that modern blackness does not present some kind of totalizing and coherent ideological framework for understanding why things are the way they are among poor, black Jamaicans. Instead, it provides a way of seeing—a double-consciousness, even—for analyzing present and future possibilities, one which exists alongside other ways of seeing, organizing, and imagining. It might be the counterpoint to the point, the reputation to the respectability, but it is as often the road not taken.[11] Still, modern blackness embodies a public power previously unattained, one that encompasses a framework for facing the everyday "double-sidedness" of Jamaica's position within the global economy. Ultimately, I am arguing that the "two-sidedness"

of modern blackness reflects the bind of its "two-sided" context—
globalization. More to the point, global capitalism—like colonialism—
has generated numerous contradictions upon which people have attempted
to capitalize in order to advance their own economic, political, and social
ambitions. These contradictions have also persisted within the realms of
cultural practice and cultural production. Winsome's play, for example,
both celebrated the culture of dancehall and recuperated aspects of the
culture of respectability. Among female DJs themselves, we hear lyrics
that destabilize the normalcy of male infidelity while others support it.
In other words, while aspects of modern blackness such as ghetto
feminism both challenge and reproduce timeworn tropes about black
vernacular culture, their constant sampling from the past also has the
potential to create something new in response to new situations. The
ongoing process of creolization, after all, not only embodies amalgamation
within a context of inequality, but also incorporates the maintenance of
an alternative set of cultural practices and values that—when they become
ascendent within the public sphere—have the potential to challenge
hegemonic hierarchies of class, color, gender, and culture.

ENDNOTES

[1] Jamaican nationalism has never been univocal. Several variants of liberal, populist, socialist, and black nationalisms have enjoyed support at various moments in Jamaica's post-emancipation period. What I am invoking here is the nationalist practice that became hegemonic within the People's National Party after the expulsion of the left wing in 1952.

[2] These are lyrics to a song entitled "Yuh Nuh Ready" by female dancehall DJ Tanya Stephens.

[3] Brian Meeks has also written that perhaps one of the ways to view the collapse of the creole multiracial nationalist project is as the collapse of a male project (1994, 133).

[4] These visions did not go unchallenged. Women, in particular, distressed the missionaries by continuing to work outside the home, as well as by playing important roles in politics (Wilmot 1995).

[5] Helen Safa has shown that contrary to popular assumptions, the male-breadwinner ideology is also as much a "myth" throughout the Spanish-speaking Caribbean as it is in the West Indies, especially given the more general economic shifts that have occurred since the late 1970s (Safa 1995).

[6] Faye Harrison, in particular, has cautioned what has emerged within popular and academic spheres as a kind of celebration of the power and autonomy of lower-class women involved in the informal sector. She writes that "despite the indisputable existence of substantial numbers of higglers, visible with the results of their mobilization of petty capital, the informal sector is not ruled by matriarchs... [W]hatever status and power individual higglers and other female retailers may in fact have within their communities, their associations, and their primary networks of kinspeople, friends, and clients, this power and status cannot be generalized to depict the situation of the majority of women in the slums and shantytowns of urban Jamaica" (1991, 189).

[7] These are lyrics to the song "Draw Fi Mi Finger" by female dancehall DJ Tanya Stephens.

[8] What I am invoking here is the "dual marriage system" as conceptualized by R.T. Smith (see R.T. Smith 1995, "Family, Social Change, and Social Policy..."; and Douglass 1992, especially pp. 238-242).

[9] This kind of discourse hasn't emerged without precedent. Several scholars have demonstrated that a consideration of women's blues during the 1920s and 1930s provides insights into the ideological debates both within and outside of the African American community during that time, and illuminates the ways working-class women contested patriarchal assumptions about "a woman's place." (See especially Carby 1999; Davis 1998; and Higginbotham 1997).

[10] Roots plays are the closest Jamaican equivalent of the African American theatre genre known as the Chitlin' Circuit. For a description of this type of cultural production in the United States, see Gates 1997.

[11] Within the U.S. context, Evelyn Higginbotham has made a similar point in her attempt to deconstruct the opposition between the blues and the church as icons of class division among African Americans (1997). She argues that during the 1920s and 1930s, the church was just as indigenous to the working poor as was the blues, and that the black poor struggled for cultural authority not only through the counterculture of

the blues, but also through the vernacular discourses of charismatic religion. This struggle, she argues, ultimately subverted the hegemonic values and aesthetic standards of the traditional Protestantism of the black middle class (1997, 158-9). As a result, the black working class emerged as the oral narrator of modernity: "Growing working-class consumerism, coupled with black middle-class disdain for the cultural styles of the poor, had initiated this important shift to working-class orality within the black public sphere" (1997, 165).

BIBLIOGRAPHY

Bilby, Kenneth. "Jamaica." In *Caribbean Currents: Caribbean Music from Rumba to Reggae*, edited by Peter Manuel, et. al. Philadelphia: Temple University Press, 1995.

Carby, Hazel. "The Sexual Politics of Women's Blues" and "Policing the Black Women's Body in an Urban Context." In *Cultures in Babylon: Black Britain and African America*, 7-21, 22-39. New York: Verso, 1999.

Chance, Clarence. "Emancipation from Dancehall Music," *Daily Gleaner*, 6 August 1997, p. A7.

Cooper, Carolyn. "Slackness Hiding from Culture: Erotic Play in the Dancehall," *Jamaica Journal* 22 (4): 12-31 (1989).

Davis, Angela. *Blues Legacies and Black Feminism: Gertrude "Ma" Rainey, Bessie Smith, and Billie Holiday*. New York: Vintage Books, 1998.

Douglass, Lisa. *The Power of Sentiment: Love, Hierarchy and the Jamaican Family Elite*. Boulder: Westview Press, 1992.

Ford-Smith, Honor. "Ring Ding in a Tight Corner: Sistren, Collective Democracy, and the Organization of Cultural Production." In *Feminist Genealogies, Colonial Legacies, Democratic Futures*, edited by Chandra T. Mohanty and M. Jacqui Alexander, 213-258. New York: Routledge, 1997.

Gates, Henry Louis. "The Chitlin' Circuit." *The New Yorker*, 3 February 1997, 44-55.

Grappo, Laura. *Ghetto Bitches and Pussy Power: A Reconstruction of Feminism*. Undergraduate Thesis, Department of English and Program in Women's Studies, Wesleyan University, 2001.

Hall, Catherine. "Gender Politics and Imperial Politics: Rethinking the Histories of Empire." In *Engendering History: Caribbean Women in Historical Perspective*, edited by Verene Shepherd, Bridget Brereton, and Barbara Bailey, 48-59. Kingston: Ian Randle Publishers, 1995.

Harrison, Faye. "Women in Jamaica's Urban Informal Economy: Insights from a Kingston Slum." In *Third World Women and the Politics of Feminism*, edited by Chandra Talpade Mohanty, Ann Russo, and Lourdes Torres, 173-196. Bloomington, IN: Indiana University Press, 1991.

Higginbotham, Evelyn Brooks. "Rethinking Vernacular Culture: Black Religion and Race Records in the 1920s and 1930s." In *The House that Race Built*, edited by Wahneema Lubiano, 157-177. New York: Vintage Books, 1997.

Meeks, Brian. "The Political Moment in Jamaica: the Dimensions of Hegemonic Dissolution." In *Radical Caribbean: From Black Power to Abu Bakr*, 123-143. Mona: The University Press of the West Indies, 1994.

Morgan, Joan. *When Chickenheads Come Home to Roost: A Hip-Hop Feminist Breaks it Down*. New York: Touchstone (A Division of Simon and Schuster), 1999.

Rose, Tricia. *Black Noise: Rap Music and Black Culture in Contemporary America*. Hanover, NH: University Press of New England, 1994.

Safa, Helen. *The Myth of the Male Breadwinner: Women and Industrialization in the Caribbean*. Boulder: Westview Press, 1995.

Smith, Raymond T. "Family, Social Change, and Social Policy in the West Indies." In *The Matrifocal Family: Power, Pluralism, and Politics*, 81-98. New York: Routledge, 1995.

Turner, Mary. *Slaves and Missionaries: The Disintegration of Jamaican Slave Society, 1787-1834*. Urbana: University of Illinois Press, 1982.

Ulysse, Gina. "Uptown Ladies and Downtown Women: Female Representations of Class and Color in Jamaica." In *Representations of Blackness and the Performance of Identities*, edited by Jean Rahier, 147-172. New Haven: Greenwood Press, 1999.

Whylie, Dwight. "The Angry Beat," *Daily Gleaner*, 14 April 1997.

Wilmot, Swithin. "'Females of Abandoned Character?': Women and Protest in Jamaica, 1838-65." In *Engendering History: Caribbean Women in Historical Perspective*, edited by Verene Shepherd, Bridget Brereton, and Barbara Bailey, 279-295. Kingston: Ian Randle Publishers, 1995.

UNDOING "HARLEMWORLD": AN ANTHROPOLOGICAL ARGUMENT ABOUT DIASPORIC DISASTERS [1]

JOHN L. JACKSON, JR.

Harlem is the most famous neighborhood in the most famous city in America. Or at the very least, that's what New York State's Visitor and Convention Bureau has been celebratorily proclaiming in its tourism literature and advertisements for the past twenty-five years. As we all know, much of this fame and notoriety rests squarely on the place's hallowed racial history as a hothouse for the flowering of a black cultural and literary "renaissance" during the roaring 1920s. The city's decade-long merriment ended gradually after the devastating stock market crash of 1929, an economic collapse that served as catalyst for the transformation of Harlem's popular reputation and representation from tempting nighttime sensation to teeming nightmarish slum.

It came to embody a place that many white New Yorkers no longer wanted to visit—and where many more wouldn't dare reside. Of course, a racially segregated housing market had blacks locked in, and as they continued to plod their way up North for a better life (from places like Georgia, Virginia, and the Carolinas), Harlem remained New York City's version of "The Promised Land," where blacks could possibly avoid the harsher injustices and inhumanities of Jim Crow segregation—and maybe even eke out a respectable living in the process. And as such, Harlem came to mean, (demographically, institutionally, and semiotically) Black Harlem. If White New Yorkers had the Great White Way of Broadway in midtown-Manhattan, African Americans, continental Africans, and Caribbeans had what some called the "Queen of all Black Belts," what many labeled the "Black Mecca," and what still others designated the "Capital of Black America." They had Harlem, U.S.A. And many of our imaginings around present-day Harlem are often little more than functional palimpsests of this hallowed past, overtures to a bygone era romanticized to excess and historical impossibility.

But, to be clear, this essay is less about Harlem than, as the title declares, Harlemworld—and with that admission, it should also be added that this piece is also a kind of meditation on nomenclatural concerns, on questions of name, naming, and renaming as processes of concretization and (as Hortense Spillers might advise) ambivalization. It tells the tale of powerful connective tissue linking choice labels and consequent actions, hewing indexical shadows, dark and murky, to the blindingly bright light of social materiality. And I highlight these issues to ask a question of the absent presences that we use to distinguish the shadow from its act—and to make an argument for an anthropological analysis that dwells within the in-between spaces that naming as cultural act with productive force opens up in our social worlds.

I want to offer up Harlemworld—the contemporary hip-hop community's name for (and renaming of) Harlem proper (that five square miles of northern Manhattan space and 300,000 persons)—as a way to mark the practical mechanics of such interconnections, a decidedly functional liminality. Of course, there are fierce political struggles and conflicts (in terms of both formal and cultural politics) that animate such connectivity. And these same struggles pit rich against poor, black against white, native against foreigner, citizen against citizen, and neighbor against neighbor in a battle for the present's future—and for victory in a much larger cultural scrimmage around what such proposed futures entail.

In January of 1996, Governor George Pataki, Congressman Charles Rangel, Mayor Rudolph Giuliani, and the Assistant Secretary for Housing and Urban Development, Andrew Cuomo, all took part in a ceremonial event organized to mark the signing of New York City's Empowerment Zone Agreement. New York would be among a handful of cities to receive block grants for community development and job creation in its depressed urban areas. Federal, state, and local governments promised $100,000,000 each, with Harlem and the South Bronx as the city's chosen sites. Harlem's new Empowerment Zone designation meant (and means) that big businesses have renewed their interest in this once-commercially-deserted area. The new influx of corporate capital has caused the value of Harlem's housing stock to soar in Manhattan's heavy-demand real estate market, increasing rental rates and housing prices higher than many current Harlemites can afford. And so, although some people notice only economic empowerment with recent Enterprise Zone initiatives, others simply see (and experience) residential displacement. It is this difference in vision that has divided this community along various fault lines, creating new social tensions between those people who gain a great deal from these changes and those who may lose it all. The unnamed space between, say, a Harlem and a Harlemworld, I believe, can tell us all a great deal about our implicit methodologies and epistemologies in theorizations of such contemporary transformations.

As urban renewal projects shift the make-up of inner-city communities nationwide, urbanites have a great deal at stake—indeed, their very lives and livelihoods. Gentrification and residential dislocation are met with tenant mobilization and "Displacement Free Zones." Amidst all of this jostling, Harlem and Harlemworld stand-in as special symbols of black urban distinctiveness, a degree of hypersymbolism that overdetermines how people make sense of themselves and their connections to others.

As an example of Harlemworld's significance, let's take the horrific acts of September 11, 2001. They changed this country forever. Almost 5,000 people were killed in both the Pentagon and the World

Trade Center. The site of the World Trade Center (WTC) is less than an hour's subway ride from 125th street, Harlem's main thoroughfare. I wrote the title for the talk on which this essay is based (*Undoing Harlemworld: An Anthropological Argument about Diasporic Disasters*) several months before the events of September 11th. Our words imply so much more nowadays than they did then. They are rife with ironies and overstatements, changed significances, and newly-wrought inappropriateness. September 11th didn't just change the tone and tenor of our collective body politic; it rewrote the semantics of our social discourse, changing our preoccupations and presuppositions about security and sociality. And so the word "disaster" has a very new meaning now, one that must be invoked carefully, respectfully, even reverently.

The nation's initial shock and fear on the 11th has gradually given way to a slightly calmer sense of continued vulnerability. American flags have become the tricolored symbol of choice for voicing patriotic resolve in the face of terrorist aggression. Children in Connecticut stuffed their quarters, nickels, and pennies into Firefighters' helmets for the relief effort. Hollywood celebrities donated seven-figure sums to the national cause. Eighteen-year-old boys in Indiana lined up at their local Army recruitment office to "fight for freedom." Even amidst all of this nationalism, however, Kevin, a nineteen-year-old African American from Harlemworld, could voice a quite different social sentiment, one that says as much about what place means to black people today as it does about African American notions of identity and community more generally:

> "I mean, look at how they've treated us," Kevin argued as he reclined in his mom's brown leather couch in an apartment building on 119th street. "Look how they've always treated us. I ain't fighting no war for them. Those people [the terrorists] ain't got no beef with me. They got beef with Bush and them, with white people. I do, too. And I ain't gonna go down there and fight them, not me. You crazy. They ain't mess with me. They ain't up in our community uninvited and whatnot. Call me when they bomb the Apollo, or one of the projects. Then I'll go fight. But don't tell me that."

Kevin's mother, who sat at the kitchen table across from her son, was mortified by his comments. A fifty-year-old office assistant who has lived in Harlem since the late 1960s, Marla first arrived from the West Indies with her two sisters when she was but a teenager. She also just so happened to work directly across the street from the World Trade Center. Her office was evacuated that morning, and she joined the mass pilgrimage of ash-covered New Yorkers forced to walk their way home on that fateful day. Marla thought that Kevin was wrong—and that he should be more than willing to enlist. She actually wanted her son to join the armed forces, to fight for this country—really, to do something, anything—as long as it was productive. Anything would be better, she thought, than his break dancing for coins in Times Square during the dead of winter—which is what he did for money last year and the year before, even before he officially dropped out of high school. And Kevin knew she felt this way. He was happy she wasn't injured, but he still drew a line in the sand over where his allegiances should rightfully stand.

She asked him how he could not see that his "Apollo" and his "projects" rested on the same material and symbolic soil as the WTC. Kevin's father is Nigerian, and so her argument turned to the marshalling of evidence about how "those people" went after the Africans first. "The same people" bombed the embassies in Africa, she almost yelled. "Where your father is from." But Kevin remained unconvinced. He was glad his mom was unharmed, he acknowledged the African connection, but he still remained skeptical. This is a skepticism, I would argue, that permeates the place. Harlemworld is soaked in it. You wonder how this skepticism would play out, say, were the World Trade Center actually in Harlem, where it quite possibly could have been, if certain advocates had had their way. There was at least a strong public push for just such a move.

In 1966, an election year, Governor Rockefeller announced that a portion of the state offices slated to be the World Trade Center would be located in Harlem, demonstrating his desire to do something for the blacks in his state (and to capture them as a voting block in his re-election bid). But many Harlem politicos and elected officials called this move little more than "crumbs to placate blacks" and lobbied for moving the entire WTC project uptown. They made passionate pleas in the black press. They held news conferences and public meetings. They wrote up proposals and opinion pieces. The State Office building that stands at 163 West 125th street now was a pared-down compromise—and even that might not have been built.

In 1968, Governor Rockefeller created the New York State Urban Development Corporation (UDC) to help rebuild certain portions of the state. The UDC overcame a political battle that threatened even the state office building project—let alone any more ambitious WTC proposal. Rockefeller found it necessary to call the state's legislators from Martin Luther King Jr.'s funeral to PR-them into signing his New York State Urban Development Act and creating the UDC, what he labeled a "super agency" for urban redevelopment. And the UDC cut through red-tape and got the State Office Building project built—even over and against public protestation about alternative uses of the space. Of course, the WTC went up, as planned, downtown, and the state office building became just a humbler twenty-story, African mask-inspired design uptown. Plans for another WTC-type building in Harlem got revived in the late 1970s, as Congressman Charles Rangel lobbied with the Harlem Urban Development Corporation (a subsidiary of the State UDC) to create the Harlem International Trade Center, which if it had ever gotten off the ground, would have doubled the size of the state office building and increased the commercial connection between African American, African, Caribbean, and Asian markets.

Amidst all the vectors of theoretical modeling possible here, to unpack the trajectories followed and not-followed in some of this brief, aforementioned Harlem history, I want to look at renaming as a vitally important lens for assisting our examination of the interesting almost-history of the World Trade Center towers uptown—and its rejuvenated and renamed promise in the form of the Harlem International Trade Center. Renaming events and things are important entry points into analyses of what we think about our worlds and ourselves.

ENDNOTES

[1] This piece is the first-half of a larger essay on naming and re-naming practices in contemporary black America. These practices are attempts at asserting selfhood and subjectivity. Here I provide some of the context for my future engagements with (re)naming as a form of racial self-empowerment.

BIBLIOGRAPHY

Anderson, Jervis. *This was Harlem*. New York: Farrar Straus & Giroux, 1982.

Jackson, John L. *Harlemworld: Doing Race and Class in Contemporary Black America*. Chicago: University of Chicago Press, 2001.

Lewis, David L. *When Harlem was in Vogue*. New York: Penguin, 1997.

Long, Jacqueline and Vernon Robinson. *How Much Power to the People?: A Study of the New York State Urban Development Corporation's Involvement in Black Harlem*. New York: Urban Center at Columbia University, 1971.

Taylor, Monique M. *Harlem between Heaven and Hell*. Minneapolis: University of Minnesota Press, 2002.

Osofsky, Gilbert. *Harlem: The Making of a Ghetto*. New York: Ivan R. Dee, Inc., 1996.

RACE, CLASS, AND CITIZENSHIP IN WESTERN EUROPE AND THE UNITED STATES

This conference explored issues of migration, identity, and ethnicity in Western Europe and the United States. Taking place in April 1997, it addressed current debates around African Diasporan identity, social class, marginalization, affirmative action, restitution, and national debates and struggles over citizenship. *Race, Class, and Citizenship* brought together the diverse experiences of faculty, community activists, and artists in the areas of human rights, social struggle, and public culture.

The conference was divided into three sessions. *Session I: The Politics of Race, Class, Identity, and Immigration* addressed cultural, social, political, and language issues as they impact the lives of "subordinately" racialized transnationals and citizens in Western Europe and the U.S. *Session II: Women and the State: Politics and Struggle in Western Europe* focused on how nations attempt to control the socioeconomic and political mobility of "subordinately" racialized transmigrant women. *Session III: Representation and Resistance in Art and Culture* was concerned with the ways in which art and public culture have been used in service of resistance and social struggle. Speakers included: Claudia Mitchell-Kernan, Scott Waugh, Baroon Saad, Lawrence Bobo, John Baugh, Cheryl Harris, M. Belinda Tucker, Richard Yarborough, Stella Dadzie, Asale Ajani, Kimberle Crenshaw, Pauline Yu, K.W. Kgositsile, John Outterbridge, Ben Caldwell, and Nikol Hodges.

—D.B.

SOCIAL CLAIMS TO PROPERTY AMONG ENSLAVED AFRICAN AMERICANS, 1850-1880

DYLAN PENNINGROTH

The relationship between slaves and property in the nineteenth-century United States seems fairly simple. Slaves were property. The "cardinal principle of slavery," according to George Stroud's 1827 summary of southern law, was "that the slave is to be regarded as a thing—is an article of property—a chattel personal." This principle, Stroud concluded, "obtains as undoubted in all of these states."[1] Because they were property, slaves could not legally own property. The relevant law in South Carolina read as follows: "[a] slave may, by the consent of his master, acquire and hold *personal* property. All, thus acquired, is regarded in law as that of the master."[2] It seems fairly straightforward for historians interested in slavery and African American life to concentrate their attention on the obvious conflict of interests between white masters and black slaves. From the slaves' viewpoint, their total lack of property completed the circle of oppression that included beatings, killings, and the threat of the slave-trader. Between master and slave, where both violence and access to resources were at stake, there was a constant antagonism. It seems equally logical to assume that the slaves constituted a community, united by their shared experience of oppression. Other than the few privileges their master might bestow, there was little at stake among individual slaves, and therefore little to divide them.

In the early 1870s, however, hundreds of former slaves—some backed by their former masters—stood before a federal compensation commission and argued that they *had* owned property as slaves. They understood perfectly well that "legally" slaves had no right to property, but they insisted that "a master who would take property from his slaves would have a hard time." According to Joseph Bacon, who lived in coastal Georgia, his master "never interfered with me and my property at all." In this paper, I am going to argue that in the nineteenth century, neither property nor the interests of the slaves were very simple at all. Some people owned property even while they themselves were property. As we look into how they were able to do this, we will begin to pry apart a seemingly unified community of slaves, and we will search the margins of the law to explore what it meant for rural people—white or black—to "own" something.

I will begin by sketching some of the ways that historians have looked at property ownership by slaves in the Americas, and then briefly summarize the overall strategy I use in my dissertation. Next, I will focus in on one example, pre-Civil War Liberty County, Georgia, to illustrate two of the themes of my dissertation. The first theme is that the South's formal institutions—law and plantation slavery—dealt with slave-owned property in complex ways. The second theme I'll discuss is that property ownership among slaves depended on informal understandings and social relationships. Lastly, I will offer some preliminary observations about slave-owned property in the South as a whole by discussing one of my main sources, the records of the Southern Claims Commission.

In the past fifteen years historians have demonstrated that in many parts of the U.S. South and the Caribbean, a significant "informal economy" existed within the formal institution of slavery, one that allowed slaves to accumulate, own, and trade property among themselves and with white people. This informal economy grew over time, out of accreted "customary" practices such as task labor (which I'll discuss in a moment). But what did it mean for slavery? What did it mean for slaves? One way to answer this question would be to ask whether the "informal economy" enabled slaves to resist the oppression of slavery. Several recent studies on the Caribbean and the American South have argued that slaves' independent economic activities helped them carve out "a measure of autonomy" away from their masters. In this view, property ownership under slavery fostered a sense of pride, "communal solidarity, and personal responsibility," qualities that, after emancipation, helped ex-slaves maintain their autonomy as a community against and apart from a new set of white landowners. Another way to see the significance of property ownership among slaves would be to treat it as an example of cultural change. Some scholars have used property ownership as a yardstick to measure "acculturation"—the cultural distance that blacks traveled away from their African roots, where there was, allegedly, no concept of individual ownership and where "everything had been held in common."[3] In sum, few studies of slave-owned property have departed substantially from two long-standing themes in African American history—the "dialectic" of accommodation and resistance, and the debate over cultural "survivals" and acculturation.

There are problems with both of these interpretations. The acculturation argument depends on four questionable, but not uncommon assumptions: first, that Africans had a clear set of values about property; second, that this system was "communal" rather than individually oriented; third, that slaves brought it to the Americas; and fourth, that their values shifted, over time, to an ethos of acquisitive individualism. These assumptions reflect twentieth-century Western thought about Africa, not eighteenth-century African values about work and property. Scholarship on pre-colonial Africa simply does not bear them out. We should use caution in creating an African baseline to sketch changes in cultural values among African Americans.

On the other hand, American historians can learn a great deal by studying Africa. African history has greatly enriched my own work on

American history. I recently did research in Accra, Ghana on property disputes among masters and slaves between the 1850s and the 1880s. Especially on the themes of slavery, kinship, and property, debates in African history have the potential to complicate and enrich American historians' work. Yet, what Frederick Cooper pointed out in 1979 is still true today, for the most part: "Africanists and Americanists are studying slavery in isolation from one another, venturing into the other's territory only to make a point about their own."[4] (My current research in Ghana is intended to bring those isolated debates into conversation with one another.)

The other approach—treating property as a form or a means of resistance to white oppression—may obscure more than it reveals. If historians now agree *that* some slaves in the American South owned property, it is still not clear *how* slaves owned property. Rather than assess American blacks' claims to property as examples of cultural change or of resistance to political and legal institutions, my dissertation concentrates on those informal understandings and practices themselves: how they were created, how they worked, and how they changed between 1850 and 1880.

Moreover, both approaches assume that, at some level, slaves' dealings with property had something to do with "autonomy." Some historians measure cultural change by assessing African Americans' eagerness to conform to classical Western economic theory—their willingness to act as autonomous economic actors. In the resistance argument, it is not so much individual slaves, but rather the slave community that strives for autonomy. Now, although it may be safe to assume that blacks sought autonomy in their dealings with whites, it does not follow that autonomy was a broadly held, broadly applicable cultural value among blacks. In fact, taking a cue from studies of Africa, I will argue that in some circumstances—especially in blacks' negotiations with one another—economic activity was predicated on social relationships, not autonomy. It may be useful to set aside any assumptions we may have about autonomy in order to scrutinize how and when people in the nineteenth century valued it or acted on it.

Although I will address only two of those questions here, my overall dissertation strategy can be briefly summarized as follows. First, I shift attention from the master-slave relationship and I make negotiations among African Americans the primary focus of my work. Second, I treat informal understandings as potentially being at least as important as formal institutions and law. Third, I draw on methodologies and perspectives from African history and anthropology. In part, this means that in examining negotiations over access to resources, I look for conflict or cooperation along lines of gender, age, and kin membership. Moreover, like many Africanist scholars, I assume that none of these categories were rigid but rather were flexible constructs, capable of responding to people's interests, including their interests in property.

What was it that gave slaves not just a chance to earn and possess property, but a remarkably stable ownership of property—at a time when they had almost no legal rights that a master was bound to respect? How relevant were law and formal institutions for people's daily lives? If slaves based their property claims outside the law, what happened to those claims after 1865, when the Union army extended the law's protection to African Americans? And if, as many scholars agree, there was an internal economy among slaves in some regions—if (in short) there *was* something at stake among slaves—then how did slaves negotiate among themselves over those resources? A whole world of social relationships and negotiations lay behind the fact that slaves owned property. That world begins to come into focus if, instead of asking, "Whose corn was it?," we pose the more fruitful question, "How did people know whose corn it was?"

Let's take a closer look at two important themes by focusing in on Liberty County, Georgia, as an example. Exactly what was the relationship between propertied slaves and the county's laws and formal plantation economy? First of all, although George Stroud knew there was a "cardinal principle" of slavery, there was no coherent body of law that one could call "the Southern law of slavery." Instead, there was a welter of state and local laws, some of them legislated, some of them judge-made. These laws tended to regulate, rather than outlaw, slaves' independent economic activity. In Georgia, for example, from the 1770s to 1830, the legislature required that slaves "shall constantly wear a Publick Badge or Ticket" when they sold "Fruit, Fish, Garden Stuff or any other Commodities whatsoever in the Town of Savannah."[5] Even Stroud's "cardinal principle" was internally inconclusive: under the law, slaves could "acquire and hold *personal* property," yet both the slaves and their property belonged to another person. Enforcing the law was another matter. People constantly violated this law and others like it, and judges' periodic attempts to enforce them simply filled the dockets of the lower courts.[6] If slaves were simply property under state law, local justice applied that principle very inconsistently. As Thomas Morris, a legal historian, put it recently, "[l]ocal practices and conditions defined the actual experience with legal rules."[7] In order to understand that experience, we must broaden our perspective to capture activities that went on outside or alongside the law.

What were those local practices that sheriffs and county judges regulated? As I mentioned before, in some parts of the South and the Caribbean, an "informal economy" existed within the formal institution of slavery. This "informal economy" allowed some slaves to accumulate, own, and trade property among themselves and with white people. In the Low Country region of coastal Georgia and South Carolina, most slaves worked under the task system, rather than the gang system that prevailed in most other parts of the South. The task system assigned each slave a certain amount of work each day—a quarter acre to hoe, for example, or a hundred wooden rails to split. The system permitted slaves to help one another in their work and allowed them to use as they wished the time left after finishing the task. By working on their own time to raise more than they needed to eat, slaves accumulated property and created traditions of property ownership and trade. Jacob Quarterman, for example, explained to a federal agent how he came to own livestock, a wagon, corn, and rice: "I bought mine sir by taking care of what little I could get."[8] At least in the Low Country, this practice of organizing labor by task rather than by time was the taproot of property ownership by slaves.

Slave-owned property and the task system were part of an important regional informal economy within the more formal economies of the plantation and the city. A former slaveowner named Edward DeLegal testified in 1873:

> I never interfered with my people, they bought & sold these things at their own prices & spent the money as they pleased & this was customary in Liberty County & I suppose it was in other seaboard counties. . . I know Mr Cay's people and mine used to raise cattle, horses, and & more [illegible] than there were any use for.

Slaves sold things along back roads and creeks to rural whites in Liberty County. They also took things to the town markets at Savannah, twenty miles away. "I brought poultry to retail in Savannah the place where I always go," testified Jacob Quarterman. "I carried it in my wagon."[9]

Not every slave owned property, and I want to emphasize that those slaves who did were making it from extraordinary amounts of overtime work. This was an economy of time, in which slaves constantly battled their masters to maintain and improve the "customary" definition of a task. Planting a personal crop meant committing to long hours of work after a hard day's task, as ex-slave Joseph James put it, "till the fowls crow for day, by moonlight and firelight."[10]

But slaves' property did not come solely from the effort and interest of individual slaves. First, planters had an interest in slaves' economic activity. By allowing slaves to grow food crops, planters effectively shifted much of the cost of subsisting their slaves onto the slaves themselves. Many masters believed that garden plots and property gave them a way to discipline their work force. Second, in order to raise and keep property, slaves very often tried to find other slaves to work for them. Testimony shows that in the Caribbean and the Low Country masters restricted slaves' access to time much more than they restricted their access to land. Masters generally allowed their slaves "all the land they could tend without rent."[11] Within this economy of time, slaves negotiated for access to other slaves' time, and they did this through kin and communal relationships, hiring, and plantation privileges. Let me concentrate on the first possibility. Slaves relied on children to help raise household property. Toney Elliott, said one witness, "had a son that helped him... worked only for his father & mother" up to the age of fifteen. Slaves were acutely aware of the value they placed on children's labor. Henry Stevens testified: "I was 30 years old before I married... my children didn't help me much. I did most of it [accumulating property] myself."[12] For slaves, raising property required joint effort, and it often meant calling on the younger members of their families to look after hogs, or tend to chickens, or help tend a crop.

Thus, alongside the formal institutions of the Low Country, slaves carried on a significant amount of economic activity. Out of an ongoing struggle between masters and slaves came informal understandings that permitted slaves to raise and trade property. But negotiations among slaves to mobilize labor were just as important as those between masters and slaves.

At the beginning of my essay I explained that legally, masters owned everything that slaves possessed. Yet, few masters took advantage of their legal rights. What kept slaves' property secure? Slaves protected their claims to property by using public occasions and public spaces to display their possessions and to secure acknowledgment from their masters and fellow slaves. Essential to this practice was the layout of the plantation's buildings and fields. Slave quarters stood in "single and double rows of cottages," according to one former slaveowner, for easy monitoring by the master. Slaves stored their belongings separately; attached to each cabin were "vegetable gardens, chicken coops, pig pens, rice ricks, and little store houses," under the control of individuals and families.[13] Ex-slaves' testimony substantiates this picture and carefully distinguishes what belonged to whom. Most of the items that ex-slaves claimed—chicken coops, beehives, hogs, produce from small gardens— were stored in their yards, where they were visible to other people. Cabins and storehouses closely adjoined, and, with three or four slaves living in each cabin, people could see from their own yards what their neighbors had. Often their display of property was more intentional. "We staid door to door to each other," testified Clarinda Lowe about her neighbor James Anderson, "& when we got any thing new we always showed one another." It is also likely that slaves gathered in their yards to socialize. If slaves frequently visited one another, the property that was cooped, penned, or stacked there would have been more or less public knowledge. Samson Bacon testifed: "I know it was his because every man on one place know every other man's property... he can't help from knowing it. All go in his yard before his door."[14] Thus, although their master designed the slave quarters with his own interests in mind, slaves used the layout to display and distinguish their property. Asking the question "Whose property was it?" captures only part of life in the Low Country. We must also ask, "How did people know whose property it was?"

Slaves sought recognition of their claims to property not just from masters but also from their spouses and their families. Marriage among slaves called for careful attention to the public dimension of personal property ownership because it rearranged the property interests of two people and their families and often split property between two households. In Liberty County, according to one slaveowner, slaves were allowed "to marry wherever they chose," but if they married off the plantation they usually were not allowed to live with their spouses. Many slaves were obliged to maintain two households, more or less complete with gardens, utensils, and all the other necessities of life. Now, on the one hand, property flowed back and forth between the households as spouses, usually husbands, shuttled between them. But the bulk of a couple's property usually remained at the wife's house. "Sometimes he would have some things at his home," said a witness in Prince Stevens' case, but only "to use up the slops of [his wife's] house." Stevens, said another witness, was known to have "lived with his wife—nights—and she took care of his property, that was the custom generally."[15] Faced with the restrictions that masters imposed on their mobility, slaves made the home—that is, the slave cabin, the multifunctional yard, and the garden—a locus of authority over property.

Uniting possessions under one roof helped secure them against threats from outside the household, but it also sparked negotiation within the household over who owned those possessions. Spouses contributed jointly the labor needed to earn property and then shared custodial responsibilities. Yet, joint effort did not rule out the possibility that in some situations slaves had an interest in asserting individual claims over property. Many of them distinguished items on the basis of who had "made" them, that is, who had contributed the labor that earned those items. However, custody could carry just as much weight in negotiations between husbands and wives who lived apart. Women were not allowed to travel as much as men and could not have controlled property that was stored elsewhere, but a woman may have been able to control and claim her husband's belongings because they were stored at her house. Men, however, could visit their wives frequently and were familiar with the property stored at their wives' homes and more often proclaimed themselves owners of it. William Cassels walked the half mile to see his wife most nights and "knew as much about my things there as at my own home." The property belonged to them both but under his expansive aegis: "[s]he doesn't claim anything separate from me we are all one." Prince Stewart testified that, although some of the things he claimed had "belonged to, and were taken from, my wife…'wesm' are all one now so I put them into my claim."[16] Married people's joint efforts to raise property and their common interest in safeguarding household property did not stop their negotiations over the control and ownership of it.

To ensure that the property interests of their children, nieces, and nephews stayed secure after marriage, some slave parents embedded that property in the public ceremony of marriage. Giving property as part of the marriage ceremony publicly affirmed the bonds between newlyweds and their relatives. But public giving also permitted the new couple to avoid confusion or hard feelings in the future by spreading knowledge about how each piece of property had come into the marriage. In this way, women may have retained some control over property. Thomas Irving, for example, did not forget that some items he claimed came into the marriage from his wife's relatives. "I got the steer by my wife," Irving testified, "her uncle made her a present of him." Jane Holmes testified: "I did not get any property by either one of my husbands… I kept the property my husband had when the raid came for his son to attend to. I had no children by him so when he died his property went to his son."[17] This careful attention to the ways property came into the marriage made each spouse's claim to ownership stronger and, to some extent, offset men's tendency to claim all household property as their own. Each spouse's relatives retained an interest in the property they gave to the couple. This practice also complicates the notion of property as the legal possession of individual owners. Each piece of property embodied the interests of several people, including the master.

The law did not recognize such ways of owning property (although principles such as "adverse possession" give them some theoretical support). By the mid-nineteenth century, American law generally assumed that property vested in individual people, and that when people transferred property, they transferred a complete bundle of rights.[18] But slaves' ownership of property did not depend on law at all, but rather on cooperative labor and custody, and the ongoing interchange of display and acknowledgment. Among Liberty County slaves, people who transferred property did not necessarily relinquish all interest in that property. Indeed, it was precisely the fact that property was enmeshed in several overlapping, sometimes competing, social relationships that made ownership possible for slaves and that made possessions into property.

How widespread and how prevalent was the ownership of property by slaves? Many scholars believe it really existed only in the Low Country, because it depended so much on the task system. In Liberty County, hundreds of ex-slaves filed claims with the Southern Claims Commission, and ninety-one of them were allowed (meaning that they won at least partial compensation). But what about other parts of the South? There are two reasons to question the assumption that property ownership by slaves was limited to the Low Country. First, a growing number of local studies have shown that slaves owned property in Upcountry South Carolina (Campbell 1993), several islands in the

Caribbean (Marshall 1993; Mintz 1974), Piedmont, Virginia (Schlotterbeck 1991), and Louisiana's sugar plantations (McDonald 1993a, 1993b).[19] Even in gang-labor economies, some slaves carved out opportunities to earn and own property. In times of high demand for workers, slaves could hire themselves out for pay, or agree to work "overtime" to earn credit against their master. Regional and international markets could cause such a spike in labor demand; so could the opening of Indian lands for settlement. Between about 1810 and 1840 eager planters dragged thousands of African Americans—and their expectations about "customary" practices—out of the Chesapeake and the Low Country to clear plantations in Alabama and Mississippi. In these "pioneer" economies planters tried, but did not completely succeed in, rolling back slaves' insistence on garden plots, personal property, and other "customary" practices.

The Southern Claims Commission provides direct evidence—if incomplete—about how many slaves owned property, and where. Congress created the Southern Claims Commission in 1871 as a way of compensating loyal unionist Southerners for property they lost to federal soldiers during the Civil War. I have surveyed the allowed claims, and my preliminary analysis suggests that slave-owned property was not confined to the Low Country. Of the nearly 5,000 allowed claims, ex-slaves filed 498, representing nearly 10% of the total. Their claims were scattered over 121 counties in every southern state except Texas and West Virginia. Free-born people of color were responsible for 231 more. An additional 104 successful claimants were slaves and became free before the Civil War. Claims by ex-slaves were not much more geographically concentrated than were claims by whites. Of the claims by ex-slaves, Georgia accounted for just under 33%, followed by Mississippi at 20%; South Carolina, Tennessee, and Alabama each accounted for about 10%. By comparison, Tennessee made up just under

25% of the allowed claims by whites, followed by Alabama at 18%, Virginia at 16%, and Georgia at 10%.

In some states, such as Alabama and Tennessee, the bulk of the claims came from whites. However, in other states, like Georgia, Mississippi, and South Carolina, more than a quarter of all the allowed claims came from former slaves. In Virginia, moreover, a substantial percentage of the state's claims were by free people of color.

These claims were not evenly spread across the states. A few counties contained unusual numbers of claims by ex-slaves; Liberty County, Georgia alone accounts for 91 of them. Were there simply more property-owning slaves in Liberty County than anywhere else? In order to understand this lumpy distribution, we must keep four other factors in mind. One is that the slave population itself wasn't evenly spread. Even in the Deep South, some counties had less than 500 slaves living in them, while in other counties more than 70% of the people were slaves. The second factor is the presence of the Union army. After all, the rules of the Southern Claims Commission said that it would only compensate people who lost property to the Union army for "legitimate army use." Many southern counties did not see much of the army. If the army did not go through a county, no one had any legitimate reason to file a claim. The third factor is the tactics the army used to get provisions. Normally, the Union army lived off of its supply lines, and did not engage in any systematic stripping of the countryside. In two significant campaigns, however—Grant's massive switchback march on Vicksburg and Sherman's march through Georgia—the Union army cut its supply lines and fed itself by foraging through the countryside. The counties with the highest number of allowed claims by ex-slaves—Liberty County, Georgia; Chatham County, South Carolina; Warren and Hinds Counties, Mississippi—sat right in the path of those two campaigns. In thinking about where in the South ex-slaves filed compensation claims, we should remember that it did not correspond exactly to where slaves had owned property before the war. Heavy concentrations of claims by ex-slaves in a few counties might simply mean that the army did unusual amounts of foraging in counties that had unusually big slave populations.

The fourth factor is that most people found it very difficult to file a claim before the Southern Claims Commission. In Liberty County, witnesses in cases frequently mentioned in passing that they, too, had lost property but had not reported it. Some of those witnesses said they had not known about the commission until after the deadline for filing. Others simply doubted that anything would come of it. Tony Law, for example, said: "I have not put in my claim against the Government yet because I haven't seen those who put in get any money. I heard that some in 'Hilton Head' had got some money but I am afraid that there won't any ever come here in my lifetime." Filing a claim cost money: both the Special Commissioner who took testimony and the claimant's lawyer charged fees and percentages that left some successful claimants with as little as $15 of an official award of $130.[20] Given the difficulty of filing, it may be that the number of claims by ex-slaves underestimates the number of slaves who had owned property.

In sum, the Southern Claims Commission contains persuasive evidence that property ownership by slaves was not just a Low Country phenomenon. Because of the large number of allowed claims outside the Low Country—especially in Mississippi—I also believe that it could flourish without the task system. When we consider the factors that had to coincide in order to generate a claim, it seems likely that the allowed claims of the Southern Claims Commission represent only a fraction of the South's enslaved property owners.

The fact that slaves owned property opens fascinating questions about slavery, southern history, and African American history. By suggesting that slaves negotiated with one another for access to resources, this argument challenges us to look beyond some of the most durable notions in scholarship on African Americans: ideas about autonomy, and of resistance—the notion of the slave community. Many scholars have recognized that African Americans placed enormous value on family and community relationships, especially in the face of physical and economic oppression by European Americans. But the evidence in the claims suggests that African Americans also negotiated among themselves over economic resources, and that social relationships were integral to such negotiation. For African American history and women's history, these negotiations offer rich opportunities to go beyond the common assumption that slave households involved an "equal partnership" between men and women, and to confront inequality and power relationships among slaves.[21] Because families provided so much of the labor it took to raise, trade, and look after property, they became a site of contestation among family members. Even as struggles between masters and slaves occurred along lines of race and legal status, other negotiations went on among slaves, and these occurred along lines of age, gender, and membership in kin groups. Such a shift in perspective invites comparisons with other regions and a productive dialogue with historians and anthropologists working on Africa.

Moreover, slavery did not mean that slaves lost all the fruits of their labor. Although the law defined them as property, slaves participated with white masters and non-slave-owning whites in an informal economy of time, land, and property that overlapped, but was largely apart from the law and other formal institutions of the South. The relationship between slaves and property was not as simple as the law's statement that slaves were property.

ENDNOTES

[1] George Stroud, A *Sketch of the Laws Relating to Slavery in the Several States of the United States of America* (1827), quoted in Thomas D. Morris, *Southern Slavery and the Law, 1619-1860* (Chapel Hill: University of North Carolina Press, 1996).

[2] John Belton O'Neall, *The Negro Law of South Carolina* (1848), quoted in Morris, *Southern Slavery and the Law, 1619-1860* (Chapel Hill: University of North Carolina Press, 1996), 350.

[3] Philip D. Morgan, "Work and Culture" and "The Ownership of Property by Slaves in the Mid-Nineteenth-Century Low Country." In *Cultivation and Culture: Labor and the Shaping of Slave Life in the Americas,* edited by Ira Berlin and Philip D. Morgan (Charlottesville: University Press of Virginia, 1993), 45, 399-420, 592; Loren Schweninger, *Black Property Owners in the South, 1790-1915* (Urbana: University of Illinois Press, 1990), 9-11, 235-36. For an extended discussion of "protopeasants," see Sidney Mintz, *Caribbean Transformations* (Chicago: Aldine, 1974), 146-55. See also Betty Wood, *Women's Work, Men's Work: The Informal Slave Economies of Lowcountry Georgia* (Athens: University of Georgia Press, 1995); *The Slaves' Economy: Independent Production by Slaves in the Americas,* edited by Ira Berlin and Philip D. Morgan (Portland: Frank Cass and Company, Ltd., 1991); and Schweninger, *Black Property Owners in the South, 1790-1915* (Urbana: University of Illinois Press, 1990), 29-60.

[4] Frederick Cooper, "Review Article: The Problem of Slavery in African Studies," *Journal of African History* 20 (1979), 103-25.

[5] "An Act To Empower Certain Commissioners," in Betty Wood, *Women's Work, Men's Work: The Informal Slave Economies of Lowcountry Georgia* (Athens: University of Georgia Press, 1995), 83.

[6] Morris, *Southern Slavery and the Law, 1619-1860* (Chapel Hill: University of North Carolina Press, 1996) 350-52.

[7] *ibid,* 226.

[8] Morgan, "Work and Culture." In *Cultivation and Culture: Labor and the Shaping of Slave Life in the Americas,* edited by Ira Berlin and Philip D. Morgan (Charlottesville: University Press of Virginia, 1993), 565-71; claim of Jacob Quarterman, p. 1, Liberty County, Georgia, Case Files, Southern Claims Commission, Records of the 3rd Auditor, Allowed Case Files, Records of the U.S. General Accounting Office, RG 217 (National Archives, Washington, DC).

[9] Testimony of Edward DeLegal in claim of Tony Axon, p. 7, *ibid;* claim of Jacob Quarterman, p. 2, Liberty County, Georgia, Case Files, Southern Claims Commission, Records of the 3rd Auditor, Allowed Case Files, Records of the U.S. General Accounting Office (National Archives, Washington, DC).

[10] Claim of Joseph James, p. 2, *ibid.*

[11] Morgan, "Work and Culture" and "The Ownership of Property by Slaves in the Mid-Nineteenth Century Low Country." In *Cultivation and Culture: Labor and the Shaping of Slave Life in the Americas,* edited by Ira Berlin and Philip D. Morgan (Charlottesville: University Press of Virginia, 1993), 14-16, 41-43, 578-79; testimony of Richard Cummings, claim of Lafayette DeLegal, in Morgan, 415; and Schweninger, *Black Property Owners in the South, 1790-1915* (Urbana: University of Illinois Press, 1990), 30-33. Woodville K. Marshall

writes that in the Windward Islands there was a "[s]cramble" among slaves "for labor services," one that "was probably more intense than the competition for land, because labor was the slaves' scarcest resource." See Woodville K. Marshall, "Provision Ground and Plantation Labor in Four Windward Islands." In *Cultivation and Culture: Labor and the Shaping of Slave Life in the Americas,* edited by Ira Berlin and Philip D. Morgan (Charlottesville: University Press of Virginia, 1993), 218.

[12] Testimony of Peter Stevens in claim of Toney Elliott, p. 9, Liberty County, Georgia, Case Files, Southern Claims Commission, Records of the 3rd Auditor, Allowed Case Files, Records of the U.S. General Accounting Office (National Archives, Washington, D.C.); claim of Henry Stevens, p. 4, *ibid.*

[13] R.Q. Mallard, *Plantation Life Before Emancipation* (Richmond: Whittet & Shepperson, 1892), 18.

[14] Average for cabin occupancy calculated from entries of 33 identifiable slaveowners, Liberty County, Georgia, 1860 Census (microfilm: M653, reel 129), Records of the Bureau of the Census, RG 29, (National Archives, Washington D.C.). Testimony of Clarinda Lowe in claim of James Anderson, p. 6, Liberty County, Georgia, Case Files, Southern Claims Commission, Records of the 3rd Auditor, Allowed Case Files, Records of the U.S. General Accounting Office; testimony of Samson Bacon in claim of Prince Stevens, p. 11, *ibid.* African Americans continued certain practices in their domestic spaces into the 1940s: they socialized and performed domestic chores in yards that were dirt rather than grass and were carefully swept with bundled sticks each day. Mary Baskerville, telephone interviews by Dylan Penningroth, Nov. 15, 1994, April 23, 1995, notes (in Dylan Penningroth's possession). See also Richard Noble Westmacott, *African-American Gardens and Yards in the Rural South* (Knoxville: University of Tennessee Press, 1992); Sidney Mintz, *Caribbean Transformations* (Chicago: Aldine, 1974), 239-49; Kate Porter Young, *Notes on Sisterhood, Kinship, and Marriage in an African-American South Carolina Sea Island Community* (Memphis, Tenn.: Center for Research on Women, 1992), 8-10; and Lydia Mihelic Pulsipher and LaVerne Wells-Bowie, "The Domestic Spaces of Daufuskie and Monserrat: A Cross-Cultural Comparison." In *Cross-Cultural Studies of Traditional Dwellings,* edited by Nezar AlSayyad and Jean-Paul Bourdier, (Berkeley: Center for Environmental Design Research, University of California at Berkeley, 1989), 1-24.

[15] R. Q. Mallard, *Plantation Life Before Emancipation* (Richmond: Whittet & Shepperson, 1892), 50-51; testimony of Samson Bacon in claim of Prince Stevens, p. 9, Liberty County, Georgia, Case Files, Southern Claims Commission, Records of the 3rd Auditor, Allowed Case Files, Records of the U.S. General Accounting Office (National Archives, Washington, D.C.).

[16] Claim of William Cassels, p. 4, Liberty County, Georgia, Case Files, Southern Claims Commission, Records of the 3rd Auditor, Allowed Case Files, Records of the U.S. General Accounting Office (National Archives, Washington, D.C.); claim of Prince Stewart, p. 2, *ibid.*

[17] Claim of Thomas Irving, p. 2, Liberty County, Georgia, Case Files, Southern Claims Commission, Records of the 3rd Auditor, Allowed Case Files, Records of the U.S. General Accounting Office (National Archives, Washington, D.C.); claim of Jane Holmes, p. 2, *ibid.*

[18] On Anglo-American conceptions of ownership and property, see Morris, *Southern Slavery and the Law, 1619-1860* (Chapel Hill: University of North Carolina Press, 1996), 61-82.

[19] John Campbell, "As 'A Kind of Freeman'?: Slaves' Market-Related Activities in the South Carolina Upcountry, 1800-1860." In *The Slaves' Economy,* edited by Ira Berlin and Philip D. Morgan (Portland: Frank Cass and Company, Ltd., 1991), 131-69; John T. Schlotterbeck, "The Internal Economy of Slavery in Rural Piedmont Virginia." In *ibid,* 170-81; Marshall, "Provision Ground and Plantation Labor in Four Windward Islands." In *ibid,* 203-20; Mintz, *Caribbean Transformations;* Roderick A. McDonald, *The Economy and Material Culture of Slaves: Goods and Chattels on the Sugar Plantations of Jamaica and Louisiana* (Baton Rouge: Louisiana State University Press, 1993).

[20] Testimony of Tony Law in claim of Linda Roberts, p. 12, Liberty County, Georgia, Case Files, Southern Claims Commission, Records of the 3rd Auditor, Allowed Case Files, Records of the U.S. General Accounting Office (National Archives, Washington, D.C.); letter from Rev. J. T. H. Waite to Charles F. Benjamin, clerk, Office of Commissioners of Claims, Feb. 1, 1877, in claim of Tony Axon, *ibid.* See also Frank W. Klingberg, *The Southern Claims Commission: A Study in Unionism* (Berkeley: University of California Press, 1955), 88.

[21] Philip D. Morgan, *Slave Counterpoint: Black Culture in the Eighteenth-Century Chesapeake and Low Country* (Chapel Hill: University of North Carolina Press, 1998), 533; Deborah Gray White, *Ar'n't I a Woman?: Female Slaves in the Plantation South* (New York: Norton, 1985), 158-59. For discussion of reluctance among women's historians to confront such inequalities, see Susan Mann, "Slavery, Sharecropping, and Sexual Inequality." In *Black Women in America: Social Science Perspectives,* edited by Micheline Malson, et al (Chicago, University of Chicago Press, 1990), 154-55.

A LOVE SUPREME:
ROMANCE, SEXUALITY, FRIENDSHIP,
AND FAMILY IN THE AFRICAN DIASPORA

FEBRUARY 9-10, 2001

A Love Supreme was an interdisciplinary event that explored the role of love in the lives of people throughout the African Diaspora. The event was based on the premise that love—in all of its forms—is a worthy topic of intellectual discourse, that it is an important force in the lives of people of all colors, and that it demands rigorous critical analysis. In addition to the conference, the event included a film festival of black love stories from throughout the African Diaspora, and a poetry reading which featured K.W. Kgositsile, Ulli K. Ryder, Kamau Daaood, Ruth Forman, Peter Harris, and Nikol Hodges.

Despite ever-changing approaches to African Diaspora research, much discourse about black experience continues to perpetuate a cultural pathology model. The *Love Supreme* conference attempted to take another step towards challenging this model as it gave participants an opportunity to document and analyze the forces that hold black communities together, as well as those that have historically torn them apart.

—D.B.

THE SWEETER THE JUICE: INTERSUBJECTIVITY AND THE EMOTIONAL POLITICS OF BLACK-ON-BLACK LOVE

DIONNE BENNETT

> ... and I really hope no white person ever has cause / to write about me / because they never understand / that Black love is Black wealth and they'll / probably talk about my hard childhood / and never understand that / all the while I was quite happy
>
> — *from NIKKI ROSA by Nikki Giovanni*

Within American youth culture, a person who "rocks you" or "rocks your world" is somebody who has seduced you so deeply, loved you so well, that life as you have known it has been shaken, shifted, eternally transformed. This metaphor, as whimsical as it may seem, hints at the potential for a mutually transformative relationship between romance and reality. This potential, if actualized, can have meaningful political and personal consequences that warrant serious investigation and analysis.

Until recently, very few scholars, with the notable exception of Franz Fanon—whose exploration of the subject in *Black Skin, White Masks* (1952) remains unrivaled in its rigor and prophetic depth— thoroughly addressed the politics of love. Most political discourse has focused on issues of wealth, power, and large-scale social change. Love has often been seen as too elusive, intimate, transient, and inconsequential to warrant serious political consideration. However, inspired by global nationalist and U.S. Civil Rights movements, many scholars of color have, over the last several decades, attempted to centralize the discussion of how love could be used to mobilize political action in much the same way that religious culture and faith have mobilized it in the past.

In this discussion of the emotional politics of love, I use the term *emotional politics* to describe the intimate relationship between power and feeling, to incite an impassioned and explicit exploration of how our discourses of power—our ideas and ideologies about the distribution of rights, responsibilities, and resources—are inextricably engaged with the way we experience, internalize, and express our emotions—our cognized and (re)cognized feelings. While my focus here is the emotional politics of African American love, my ultimate goal is to encourage and participate in a larger analysis of the emotional politics of race within a range of contexts and conditions.

The fact that love is a political emotion is exposed by the relentless failure of Western culture to acknowledge it as being in any way relevant to people of color. Over fifty years ago, Zora Neale Hurston commented on the implications of this failure, this negation of the emotional capacities of non-white people, in her essay "What White Publishers Won't Print" (1950), in which she lamented "the lack of literature about the higher emotions and love life of upper-class Negroes and the minorities in general" (Hurston 1989, 170). Hurston, not only describes the dilemma of the emotional erasure of African Americans, but links it to America's cultural construction of "nation" in a global context:

> National coherence and solidarity is implicit in a thorough understanding of the various groups within a nation, and this lack of knowledge about the internal emotions and behavior of the minorities cannot fail to bar out understanding (Hurston 1989, 169).

This lack of understanding is observed not merely by outsiders, but often extends to our relationships with each other and has direct and powerful repercussions for a range of dynamics between Black men and women. As Cornel West explains:

> The very notion that Black people are human beings is a new notion in Western Civilization... one of the consequences of this pernicious idea is

that it is very difficult for Black men and women to remain attuned to one
another's humanity (hooks & West 1991, 12).

Hurston, and later West, realized that the refusal to recognize the emotional
lives of people of color is more than an ethnocentric oversight; it is way
of dehumanizing us. If the ability to experience complex emotion is, in
fact, an index of one's humanity, then the will to claim that ability is a
form of resistance against dehumanizing forces. The negation of Black
people's capacity to love is directly related to the perception that we lack
the humanity necessary to experience love—that we do not know what
love is or how to express it—and that we do not deserve to be loved
even by each other.

Yet, we as African Americans know not only that we are capable
of loving each other, but that this love has been a force that has sustained
us in the face of countless tragedies, including the Trans-Atlantic slave
trade—one of the most hateful and dehumanizing practices in world
history. In a talk she gave at Yale University in 1987, the late Toni Cade
Bambara theorized that the African American concern with romantic
love—which can be observed in almost every form of African American
cultural production, particularly in music, literature, and film—is directly
related to the degree to which romantic love was punished and repressed
during slavery. Because all forms of emotional attachment between
slaves were threatened by the policy of ruthlessly separating slaves
regardless of their kinship or emotional bonds, Bambara speculated that
romantic love, while certainly practiced by slaves, was emotionally
dangerous—a source of anguish as well as endurance. Therefore, when
we had the freedom to love each other without restraint we indulged that
freedom passionately.

However, in academic discourse the fervent interest of millions
of African Americans in the subject of love is often ignored or dismissed.
Yet, this seemingly most personal of all emotions has meaningful political

implications and consequences. Our challenge, though, is to go beyond the long-heard assertion that "the personal is political." Instead, we might explore how our personal politics and our social politics, our intimate bonds as well as our devotion to community—while different in scope and meaning—might engage, respond to, and enrich one another.

Identity, Intersubjectivity, and Emotional Politics

Successful love relationships and successful resistance movements share some essential paradigms with one another. One of these paradigms is the will to subvert the Eurocentric binarisms—particularly social, political, and cultural manifestations of the "self/other" or "subject/object" construct—that are so frequently at the core of white, Western representations of identity. Within that model the white, the male, the wealthy, the heterosexual, the young, the educated, the healthy occupy the "subject" category while the black, the female, the poor, the gay, the old, the very young, the under-educated, the ill, and disabled occupy the "object" category. Almost as destructive as the social practices that maintain the forces of white supremacy, patriarchy, homophobia, classism, ageism, etc., is the cultural assumption that dynamics of domination are natural, inevitable, and unchangeable.

On an interpersonal level, one of the fundamental flaws in the representation of the self/other dyad is the idea that this opposition—the dynamic of dominance—is inherent to all social interaction. All experiences of love challenge that construction, open up the possibility of a self/self or subject/subject dynamic that engages one's humanity so totally that it "rocks your world" in completely new and mutually empowering ways. Indeed, part of the power of love lies in its ability to dismantle traditional, and oppressive, social norms of experience.

Therefore, contrary to most other social dynamics in western culture, love is a self/self relationship characterized by what feminist psychologist Jessica Benjamin describes as "intersubjectivity" (Benjamin 1988) which refers to the dynamic and dialogic interaction between mutually recognized subjects. The term *intersubjectivity* is embedded in both philosophical and psychoanalytic theoretical traditions and can provide a useful paradigm for making political assessments of truth and meaning as well. Benjamin uses the term to describe a healthy mother-child relationship by writing:

> The intersubjective view maintains that the individual grows in and through the relationship to other subjects. Most important, this perspective observes that the other whom the self meets is also a self, a subject in his or her own right. It assumes that we are able and need to recognize that other subject is different and yet alike, as an other who is capable of sharing similar mental experience. Thus the idea of intersubjectivity reorients the conception of the psychic world from a subject's relations to its object toward a subject meeting another subject (Benjamin 1988, 30).

Understanding that the self/other relationship is not the only option for social interaction is central to understanding the kinds of alternative social options that emotion makes available to us. It is precisely this longing for intersubjectivity that links the emotion of love with political practices of empowerment. Both argue that domination is *not* the only model of personal or political interaction. Both strive to achieve a radical intersubjectivity that is achieved when two autonomous subjects (as opposed to individuals or groups who occupy a subject/object relationship or an object/object bond) recognize each other, acknowledge the differences between them, and are willing to learn from these differences and to grow together into the space between them.

If we are, as I suspect, in a sort of racial and sexual cold war against oppressions so insidious, so frequently invisible and inaudible, so callously covert, and so relentless that we often have trouble explaining them even to ourselves, then the practice of intersubjectivity is a form of emotional, intellectual, and political training that will serve us well in all battles—acknowledged and denied. More importantly, the practice of intersubjectivity will enhance the quality of our relationships and our everyday lives, a practice that is, in many ways, our greatest form of resistance.

Romanticizing Politics and Politicizing Love

It is essential not only that we recognize the similarities between emotional and political intersubjectivity—between love and empowerment—but also that we recognize the powerful impact that each can have on the achievement of the other. Again, many thinkers who focus on the large-scale political forces that shape our lives might consider a focus on love to be a trivialization of both those forces and of the people whose lives are dominated by them. Yet, love is not a trivial matter in the daily lives of individuals who are the subjects of sophisticated political discourses. For most of us, love is important, meaningful, powerful, and intensely real.

Life, whether we admit it or not, is a highly emotional enterprise. Oppression is an unfortunate part of this enterprise and has intense emotional repercussions. While those who focus on oppression may believe that they are simply ignoring the unimportant when they fail to discuss the emotional politics of oppression, they may simply be failing to explicitly identify the emotions that are actually at the root of most political practices. Oppression and all of it its offspring: discrimination; violence; abuse; and inadequate food, housing, education, health care, and opportunity have emotional repercussions, which include self-hatred, shame, doubt, despair, and fear. These emotions are powerful, insidious, pervasive, and unavoidable. Yet, they are not the only emotional politics involved in the experience of oppression.

Oppression and the representations of its emotional repercussions can be described as the politics of suffering. The practice and celebration of love are essential to a meaningful politics of resistance. The late activist and educator Paolo Freire eloquently advocated for the critical role love must play in progressive political life when he stated:

> I am more and more convinced that true revolutionaries must perceive the revolution, because of its creative and liberating nature, as an act of love. For me, the revolution, which is not possible without a theory of revolution—and therefore science—is not irreconcilable with love... The distortion imposed on the word "love" by the capitalist world cannot prevent the revolution from being essentially loving in character, nor can it prevent the revolutionaries from affirming their love of life (Paolo Freire, 1970).

Freire is a powerful model for addressing resistance in explicitly emotional terms and centralizing love within political discourse. Yet, when the emotional politics of oppression are addressed, it is the emotion of rage that is most commonly recognized as being linked to agency and social transformation. As Freire indicates, love could function as one of the most effective forms of resistance precisely because, like anger, it is so powerful and because it is often profoundly enduring in ways that many other emotions are not.

Furthermore, love may be a more compelling tool of long-term political transformation than traditional forms of resistance. Bell hooks critiques the limits of resistance by describing resistance as merely "acting against." She instead advocates for participating in the process of "becoming subjects" through the process of developing a critical consciousness (hooks 1990, 33). For political activists, love can function both as source of subjectivity and one of the most inspiring and enduring forms of resistance. Hooks explains that:

We need to concentrate on the politicization of love, not just in the context of talking about victimization in intimate relationships, but in a critical discussion where love can be understood as a powerful force that challenges and resists domination. As we work to be loving, to create a culture that celebrates life, that makes love possible, we move against dehumanization, domination... (hooks 1989, 26).

The depoliticization of emotion has repercussions not only for the objects of oppression but also for those who have been charged with perpetuating it. In both academic and popular culture those who perpetuate oppression are often represented as being emotionless while, in reality, they are just as emotionally involved as objects of oppressive practices. Indeed, they often display an intense emotional investment in the form of ferocious denial.

I am not suggesting that progressive thinkers deny that racism, sexism, classism, heterosexism, xenophobia, etc. are powerful institutional forces that are frequently characterized by a total disregard, on the part of perpetrators, for the humanity of their victims. However, I would argue that these are institutions that are perpetuated and negotiated by human beings. We often speak of these human beings as if they were mechanized agents of forces of domination. What we fail to discuss is that agents of domination are successful not because they are emotionless, but because they manage to exploit the emotions of the people whom they are controlling.

While the politics of suffering must be addressed compassionately and thoroughly, we must also explore alternative ways of being emotionally, just as we explore alternative ways of being politically. It is imperative that more African Americans who wish to participate in struggle focus on the variety of emotions, elements, and forces that make political struggle a source of pleasure, joy, and empowerment. This is a potentially spirit-sustaining alternative to our frequent policy of treating struggle as a practice that we merely endure until liberation finally arrives or ignore because we, cynically, believe that it never will.

While some thinkers focus exclusively on the politics of suffering, others deny the degree to which the process of politicization can be excruciatingly painful. We are so inundated with emotional propaganda that suggests that we "Wake Up!" and "the truth will set you free," we sometimes forget the reality that the truth will also break your heart. The failure of many contemporary political movements emerges from the fact that so many of us simply cannot stand the pain. Love theorists attempt to teach us that love can make the pain bearable.

During her lifetime, visionary poet and activist Audre Lorde saw love as an important political strategy for tending the extraordinary wounds that characterize political struggle. She explains:

> The very word *erotic* comes from the Greek word *eros,* the personification of love in all its aspects... [it provides] the power which comes from sharing deeply any pursuit with another person. The sharing of joy, whether physical, emotional, psychic, or intellectual forms a bridge between the sharers, which can be the basis for understanding much of which is not shared between them and lessens the threat of their difference. Recognizing the power of the erotic within our lives can give us the energy to share genuine change within our world (Lorde 1984, 57-58).

Here Lorde explores the larger political implications of Benjamin's assertions regarding our need for mutual recognition. In a sense, Lorde is suggesting love as an emotional plan of intersubjective action. Such a plan involves at least two forms of intersubjective recognition: one in which similarities of sensibilities, experiences, connections, etc. are acknowledged, celebrated, and utilized as the raw materials for building "a bridge across differences," and the other in which differences of opinion, emotion, background, perception, etc. are crossed on that bridge of recognized similarities, so that these differences can be acknowledged, accepted, and ideally provide a source of education. Moreover, Lorde sees love and the erotic as critical to envisioning a liberated culture, and therefore critical to making such a culture possible.

Those who are truly invested in the goal of what N'gugi Wa Thiongo calls "decolonizing the mind" must be equally invested in decolonizing the heart. We must do more than focus on the coldest realities of the lives of the oppressed, we must celebrate that oppression has a limit, a boundary it cannot cross, and that boundary is marked emotionally through our bonds with each other. Love is not an elite emotion nor a frivolous one. People of all cultures and classes take the time to think about love, to worry about love, to create love because it is important and redemptive. Love is not only a powerful presence in the lives of those who suffer through the forces of political oppression; it is a presence that makes survival possible.

Ethical Ambition and Ethical Emotion: Just Love

Our emotions are the measure of our ethical conflicts and mark the parameters of the cultural values that shape them. Our feelings tell us what we know, what we value, and what we must do. Ambition, then, marks not only our desire for power, but our desire for the moral legitimacy of the powers we seek—whether they are economic, political, or emotional. I challenge us to think in terms of ethical ambition—or morally-motivated desire—so that we do not merely claim our desires, but attempt to consciously shape them in the image of our ethics. Here I am describing ethics not merely as values since so many of our values ruthlessly compete with each other—*Do I want true love or do I want someone who can really cook?* I present ethics as our *best* values, the values we hope will win these competitions that take place so relentlessly in our heads.

Do note that I am not suggesting a negation of ambition itself. Our ambitions are useful sources of information and motivation. Furthermore, in our consumer culture, such a suggestion is nothing less than absurd. However, reshaping our ambitions according to our ethics —our best values—both increases the likelihood that our ambitions will be fulfilled and decreases the emotional anguish that emerges, not only when our ambitions fail, but when they inspire as much shame over their moral compromises as they do desire for their fulfillment.

Ethical ambition is the moral map of love; it is a guide for the practice of intersubjectivity on both intimate and social levels. Its goal is very clear: Integrity — both as moral justice and as meaning-producing wholeness. Ethical ambition takes the emotional politics of love and elevates them to the level of moral policy. In order for the emotional politics of love to function in a meaningful way on anything like a grand social scale, we must experience equally grand ethical ambitions for our communities, our cultures, our world. When our political goals are fueled by a combination of love (intersubjective practices) and ethical ambition (a matrix of morally-motivated desires)—we simply cannot and will not be satisfied by the absurd compromises we have been compelled to accept or by the equally absurd aspirations that reduce us all to the level of either concept or commodity. In other words, we can address our meaningful political goals while remaining vigilantly aware that we are more—much more—than the social categories we represent and the things that can be done to and with them.

The most dangerous aspect of amoral ambition, desire that lacks ethical motivation, is that our ambitions are not merely for more power, more money, and more toys; our ambitions extend to people—to our desires for more attractive, more successful, more impressive romantic partners than many of us feel we have access too. Black men and women need solutions to our emotional, social, and economic challenges that are sensitive to the cultural context in which they occur and the cultural values that we cherish. At the same time, we need to be aware that we are harboring cultural values that are dehumanizing and destructive to ourselves and each other. The internalization of racist, sexist, and classist ways of thinking about and interacting with each other are among these.

For example, Black women of all classes and sexualities, regardless of how we look, are often made to feel that our failure to conform to white supremacist beauty standards compromises our desirability as romantic partners. Black men of all classes and sexualities, regardless of how hard they work, are often made to feel economically undesirable. The challenge is not merely for us all—including women— to measure women's worthiness beyond our bodies and for us all—including men— to measure men's worthiness beyond their wallets. The challenge is to practice ethical ambition and ethical emotion, to redesign our desires according to our values, particularly our political values. This means privileging the values that celebrate our culture, subjectivity, and humanity over our desire to "win" a racist and sexist game that is rigged against us from birth and could only make a handful of wealthy, straight, white men truly happy—and that's only if they are pathologically shallow. If we claim that "Black is Beautiful," but only aesthetically affirm high yella women, or acknowledge that racism effects Black unemployment, but submit men to the message of the song, "Hit the Road, Jack" which claims: "You got no money, you just ain't no good" —we are missing not only the point; we are also, very tragically, missing each other.

We must work as hard for love—ethical, passionate, intersubjective, and whole love—as we work for beauty and money. If we can allow the media, in the time it takes to air a commercial or music video, to sell us desires for millions of dollars worth of products that we do not and will not *ever* need, then why do we hesitate to take the time and energy to sell each other—and particularly our children—on the desire for healthy, egalitarian, intersubjective bonds with individuals who may not meet media standards of beauty and wealth, yet meet, or far exceed, the ethical standards of our own minds, spirits, and hearts. We need these bonds, we need them badly, and it would be a great political victory for us to truly desire each other *as we are* as fervently as we desire new cars, new clothes, new hairstyles, and new partners.

I encourage African Americans to practice ethical ambition—to question, challenge, and reform our desires according to our moral and political values—so that we get into the cognitive habit of feeling an entire range of ethical emotions about ourselves and each other—ethical fear, ethical rage, ethical joy, ethical hope, etc. By making our ethical codes emotional, as well as intellectual, and by feeding our desires with our values instead of our vanity, we increase the possibility that love will be recognized as an accessible, achievable daily practice rather than an unobtainable ideal.

If the African American community is going to survive what many consider a "Black love crisis"—which is inextricably linked to the alleged "crisis in the black family"—we are going to have to use the tools that this crisis has given us in order to dig our way out of it. As we consider solutions to the love crisis in the Black community, it is essential to remember that black men and women are forging meaningful, but flawed, emotional bonds. We are not starting with nothing and nowhere. We are starting with confused longings in a place of disappointed expectations where we have been guided by misunderstood actions. Not an ideal beginning, but a place of hope, possibility, and hard-won wisdom. In fact, it is our deep emotional investment in one another that can be the source, not only of broken hearts and wounded spirits, but also courage, trust, and vision. If Black psyches, families, and communities are to survive, Black men and women must take seriously the responsibility for healing ourselves both individually and together. In the end, I predict that it will only be our faith in each other, in our culture, in our communities, and in love itself that will sustain and nurture us.

BIBLIOGRAPHY

Bambara, Toni Cade. Lecture. Yale University. 1987.

Benjamin, Jessica. *The Bonds of Love: Psychoanalysis, Feminism, and the Problem of Domination.* New York: Pantheon Books, 1988.

Cade, Toni, ed. *The Black Woman: An Anthology.* New York: Signet Classics, 1970.

Fanon, Frantz. *Black Skin, White Masks.* (1952) New York: Grove Press, 1967.

Freire, Paolo. *Pedagogy of the Oppressed.* New York: Herden & Herden, 1970.

Hooks, bell. *Yearning: Race, Gender, and Cultural Politics.* Boston: South End Press, 1990.

Hooks, bell and Cornell West. *Breaking Bread: Insurgent Black Intellectual Life.* Boston: South End Press, 1991.

Hurston, Zora Neale. *I Love Myself When I Am Laughing ... And Then Again When I Am Looking Mean and Impressive: A Zora Neale Hurston Reader*, edited by Alice Walker. New York: The Feminist Press, 1989.

Lorde, Audre. *Sister Outsider.* Freedom, CA: The Crossing Press Feminist Series, 1984.

Stevenson, Brenda E. "Black Family Structure in Colonial and Antebellum Virginia: Amending the Revisionist Perspective." In *The Decline of Marriage Among African-Americans,* edited by Belinda M. Tucker and Claudia Mitchell-Kernan. New York: Russell Sage Foundation, 1995.

Tucker, M. Belinda and Claudia Mitchell-Kernan, eds. *The Decline of Marriage Among African Americans.* New York: Russell Sage Foundation, 1995.

Wyatt, Gail Elizabeth. *Stolen Women: Reclaiming Our Sexuality, Taking Back Our Lives.* New York: John Wiley & Sons, Inc, 1997.

THE AFRICAN DIASPORA RESEARCH COALITION

The African Diaspora Research Coalition (ADRC) is an interdisciplinary work-group for graduate students (and invited undergraduates) who conduct research in the African Diaspora. It was formed by CSADP graduate students in collaboration with UCLA's Black Graduate Student Association. The group was designed to encourage graduate students to: move quickly and successfully through their academic programs; maintain their research and writing schedules; and exchange productive feedback on their work with a group of informed and supportive peers. The primary activity of the ADRC involved student presentations of work for dissertations, master's theses, qualifying exams, articles, and conferences. Additional activities included: progress check-ins; problem-solving workshops; essential African Diaspora text discussions; and future work commitment planning. During its first year, the ADRC conducted application-writing workshops for students applying to Ph.D. programs or fellowships. The results were remarkably successful. Every single student who participated in the workshops was admitted to a prestigious Ph.D. program or received the fellowships for which they applied.

The ADRC developed a dynamic intellectual community for its participants. Although the CSADP reached its conclusion in 2002, the ADRC continues to meet and will serve as one of the legacies of the CSADP. Ultimately, the group hopes to support a new generation of African Diaspora scholars who intellectually nurture and inspire each other in a *noncompetitive* manner and who are united both by their passion for African Diaspora research and their political commitment to fighting oppression with knowledge, integrity, and community.

Following are excerpts of essays from graduate students who have been involved in the CSADP over the years. These essays document the range of subjects and disciplines explored by UCLA graduate students who have chosen the rewarding field of African Diaspora research.

—D.B.

SPREADING THE GOSPEL OF DEMOCRACY: ATHLETICS, RACE, AND THE COLD WAR

DAMION THOMAS

Between 1945 and 1968, 117 sports teams, 535 athletic coaches, and hundreds of other individuals were sent to nations in Africa, Asia, the Near East, Far East, and South America under the State Department's Goodwill Tours Programs. The four-fold purpose of the programs was to demonstrate American mastery of various sports; to teach the latest sports techniques to foreign athletes as they prepared for national, regional, and international sports competitions; to provide arenas for mutual understanding and friendships to flourish between athletes and countries; and to champion the American capitalist, democratic way of life. Situated in an historical epoch when crucial issues surrounding integrated sports, race, anti-colonialism, Civil Rights, and the Cold War coalesced, the United States employed athletics in their propaganda campaign because they were highly visible, cost effective, and attractive to a broad mass of people. More importantly, however, athletics' subtlety and assumed inherent lack of ideological content minimized sports' vulnerability to the charges of neo-colonialism and cultural imperialism that plagued other American propaganda efforts.

One of the State Department's most successful tours involved Mal Whitfield, an African American middle distance runner. Mal Whitfield had sneaked into the Los Angeles Coliseum and witnessed Eddie Tolan's victory over Ralph Metcalfe in the 100 meter final at the 1932 Olympic Games. Whitfield credits that moment with inspiring him to achieve Olympic gold. Whitfield's dreams came true at the 1948 Olympic Games, when he won gold medals in both the 800 meter and 1600 meter relays, while taking home a bronze medal in the 400 meter dash. He followed that performance with an impressive showing at the 1952 Olympics in Helsinki: a gold medal in the 800 meter dash and silver medal in the 1600 meter relay. Whitfield, who throughout his career established sixteen world records, became the first African American to be awarded the Amateur Athletic Union's James E. Sullivan Award as America's outstanding amateur athlete of 1954.

In addition to his athletic accomplishments, Mal Whitfield had displayed his loyalty to the United States during the Korean War where, as a Second Lieutenant, he flew twenty-seven combat missions. Because of his athletic accomplishments and his military service, it was no surprise when the State Department asked Mal Whitfield in 1954 to take an international tour under its American Specialist Program to "enhance U.S. prestige… and assist in creating an atmosphere favorable to the acceptance of American friendship, goodwill, advice, and possible assistance." His itinerary contained nine destinations: Belgrade, Yugoslavia; Lagos, Nigeria; Accra, Gold Coast; Karachi, Dacca, and Lahore, Pakistan; Rangoon, Burma; Athens, Greece; and Nairobi, Kenya.[1]

While abroad, Whitfield maintained a hectic schedule conducting clinics, participating in exhibitions, showing films, and giving lectures. For example, during his stay in Karachi he spoke before twenty-four different audiences: nine colleges and universities; two groups of instructors and athletes from approximately fifty high schools; three groups of Royal Army, Navy, and Air Force groups; and ten other mixed groups with an additional twelve receptions, luncheons, and dinners in his honor. The Karachi embassy estimated that he personally addressed 11,500 local Pakistani citizens. His stop in Rangoon was also frenzied: he conducted four clinics, ran in a track meet, and spoke at several dinners in his honor.[2]

Whitfield's enthusiasm and hard work stemmed from his belief in the importance of sports as a vehicle for fostering peace. "Atom bombs cannot establish peace in the world, but goodwill visits of this kind are the only medium by which free and freedom loving people can hope to bring peace to the world," Whitfield stated in Accra. Undoubtedly, he shared the State Department's view that athletics could help improve international goodwill.

The seemingly apolitical character of the tour also helped consolidate and expand contacts in the athletic field, thereby helping reach segments of the various nations' population "that were not so receptive to other USIS (United States Information Services) activities." The Public Affairs Officer at Dacca, Fentress Gardner, expressed a similar sentiment in her report about the track star's visit: "Dacca could use more visitors of this type, particularly of the young enthusiasts who are successful in their own field and who appeal to certain groups of students who are difficult to reach in other ways."[3]

The State Department was most interested in how United States race relations were contextualized on the tour. At a lecture in a downtown theater in Athens in mid-January 1955 before a crowd of four hundred, Whitfield's address highlighted sacrifice, hard work, team spirit, and determination as essential ingredients to championship performances, and the idea that athletics could bring peace, health, and contentment to the world. The embassy report noted that "the lecture itself was not impressive. It had obviously been prepared for any and every occasion, and had not been adapted to the local situation in any way." However, Whitfield was quite engaging during question-answer segments particularly on questions involving United States race relations. For example, he was asked why the Sullivan Award Committee did not honor Jesse Owens after his four gold medal performance at the 1936 Olympics. The American Embassy was pleased to report that Whitfield "deftly turned his reply into a review of the immense progress made in the United States… toward race tolerance." He referred to his own selection as the 1954 Sullivan awardee as evidence that the United States was moving "toward a final solution of the problem of race relations."[4]

Mal Whitfield's personal success as an African American was crucial to achieving his mission to alter international perceptions of the United States. His subtlety in addressing the United States' racial dilemmas caught the attention of Joseph C. Kolarek, the Public Affairs Officer at the American Embassy in Belgrade, Yugoslavia. At a cocktail party where Whitfield met Yugoslav athletic leaders and athletes, he answered questions in a manner that was "of considerable propaganda value," according to Kolarek, the host of the party. By pointing out that the United States was a large nation with regional interests and attitudes about different sports and various other aspects of American life, he "indirectly but effectively made the point that the Negro problem in the United States is regional rather than national," claimed Kolarek. As a world-renowned athlete, Whitfield's advice and judgement were respected by the athletic community, coupled with his "hard-working, assured, and level-headed" demeanor. Kolarek was led to judge Whitfield's visit as an "unqualified success."[5]

Several years later in 1957, Mal Whitfield was again asked by the State Department to take another tour of North and East Africa: Tunis, Tunisia; Tripoli, Libya; Nairobi, Kenya; Kampala, Uganda; Monrovia, Liberia; and Freetown, Sierra Leone. The tour was successful, but Whitfield had to overcome several setbacks: schools were closed for summer vacation; in Tunis, Whitfield suffered an ankle sprain that hindered his ability to compete; and a case of the flu put him on bed rest in Monrovia. Because of the ankle sprain, he was limited to lecturing, but the State Department was satisfied with the connections that he helped to foster with several target groups: athletic clubs, teachers, army personnel, and police officials.[6]

Whitfield faced a hectic schedule to maximize his brief visit. For example, while in Libya on July 18, 1957, he began his day with a lecture and demonstration to the Libyan police cadets at 8:30 a.m. and concluded with a 9:30 p.m. film session and talk to an athletic club. He was received with enthusiasm because he estimated that he could help his target groups develop a regular sports training program, if he could stay there for three months.[7] He was so convinced of the ability of sports to help foster harmonious social relationships that after he finished his athletic career he became an administrator for the State Department athletic tours in Africa, and dedicated himself to improving athletic skills on the continent.

The Community Development Sports Officer in Nairobi, R.H.W. Batchelor, was so impressed with Whitfield's work in that city, he wrote that Whitfield possessed "the gift of spreading the gospel of Democracy and Christianity through the medium of Athletics." An injury hindered Whitfield from competing at a meet, but the disappointed crowd was treated to his expert instruction. He demonstrated his personal, practical workout. He playfully pointed out several common faults that track athletes made; his energy and enthusiasm "had the crowd in fits of laughter." Thereafter, he showed how these faults could be remedied. His presentation earned a rousing ovation. Whitfield was at his best when working directly with the athletes. His excitement was infectious as he tried to help the athletes develop perfect technique. His influence was evident as participating athletes set ten new records at the Coast Championships held in Mombasa. The local communities openly gave Whitfield the credit for the improved performances.[8]

Mal Whitfield's second tour helped generate goodwill towards the United States on several fronts: America was praised for taking an interest in the success and development of the nations involved in the tours and he demonstrated the improving place of the African American in American society. Records were broken everywhere that Whitfield conducted clinics. Howard Russell, an officer at the American embassy in Nairobi said that even more important than Whitfield's athletic accomplishments were his "friendliness and willingness to do anything requested of him which made friends for him and for the United States throughout the country. He cheerfully worked twelve to fourteen hour days and seven-day weeks without a single complaint. His effectiveness could hardly be exaggerated." William C. Powell, the Public Affairs Officer at the Monrovia American embassy, said that Whitfield helped improve Liberian appreciation of African American advancement because he was "a representative American Negro whose contribution to the American way of life is recognized throughout the world."[9]

The politics of token symbolism associated with Whitfield's tours and other tours by African American athletes were designed to give legitimacy to existing racial inequalities in American society during the Cold War/Civil Rights Era. The symbol of the integrated athlete allowed the government to argue that segregation was not an impediment to the advancement of individual African Americans. Whitfield's success symbolized before the world the accessibility of "the American Success Myth" for African Americans; thereby propagating the notion that talented and motivated African Americans could succeed in American society despite racial obstacles.

ENDNOTES

[1] "American Specialist Program— Report on Mal Whitfield's Visit to East Africa," American Consulate in Nairobi, January 30, 1958 National Archives (NA), 032 Whitfield, Mal/1-3058; Ron Fimrite, "A Call to Arms. (Athletes in World War II)," *Sports Illustrated* v75, n18 (Fall, 1991), 98-103; "American Specialist Program—Mal Whitfield," March 1, 1957, NA, 032 Whitfield, Mal/3-157; "Visit of Mal Whitfield to Liberia and Sierra Leone," American Embassy Monrovia, October 4, 1957, NA, 032 Whitfield, Mal/10-457.

[2] "U.S. Specialists Program— Mal Whitfield," American Embassy Karachi, January 5, 1955, NA, 511.90D3/1-555; "U.S. Specialist Program," American Embassy Rangoon, January 14, 1955, Bureau of Educational and Cultural Affairs (CU), Box 93, Folder 8.

[3] "Visit of Mal Whitfield," American Embassy Athens, January 2, 1955, CU, Box 93, Folder 8; "Visit of U.S. Specialist— Mal Whitfield," United States Information Service (USIS) Dacca, January 13, 1955, NA, 511.003/1-1355.

[4] "U.S. Specialist Program— Mal Whitfield," American Embassy Accra, October 29, 1954, CU, Box 93, Folder 8; "Report on the Visit of Mal Whitfield to Kenya on the 18th of January, 1955," American Embassy Nairobi, undated, CU, Box 93, Folder 8; "Visit of Mal Whitfield," American Embassy Athens, January 2, 1955, CU, Box 93, Folder 8.

[5] "U.S. Specialists' Program— Mr. Mal Whitfield," USIS Belgrade, January 18, 1955, CU, Box 93, Folder 8.

[6] "American Specialist Program— Mal Whitfield," March 1, 1957, NA, 032 Whitfield, Mal/3-157; "Visit of American Specialist, Mal Whitfield," American Embassy Tripoli, July 27, 1957, NA, 032 Whitfield, Mal/7-2757; "Visit of Mal Whitfield to Liberia and Sierra Leone," American Embassy Monrovia, October 4, 1957, NA, 032 Whitfield, Mal/10-457.

[7] "Visit of American Specialist, Mal Whitfield," American Embassy Tripoli, July 27, 1957, NA, 032 Whitfield, Mal/7-2757.

[8] "American Specialist Program—Report on Mal Whitfield's Visit to East Africa," American Consulate Nairobi, January 30, 1958, 032 Whitfield, Mal/1-3058; "American Specialist Program—Report on Mal Whitfield's Visit to East Africa," American Consulate Nairobi, October 29, 1957, NA, 032 Whitfield, Mal/10-2957.

[9] "US Specialist Mal Whitfield's Program in Uganda," USIS Kampala, October 9, 1957, NA, 032 Whitfield, Mal/2-1342.

"A PANIC IN ALL THIS COUNTRY": NAT TURNER'S COMPLEX AND DYNAMIC RELIGIOUS BACKGROUND [1]

JAKOBI WILLIAMS

As we came back the way that Nat led his army,
Down from Cross Keys, Down to Jerusalem,
We wondered if his troubled spirit still roamed the Nottaway,
Or if it fled with the cock-crow at daylight,
Or lay at peace with the bones in Jerusalem,
Its restlessness stifled by Southampton clay.[2]

—Sterling Brown

Scholar Peter H. Wood has noted in his article, "Nat Turner: The Unknown Slave As Visionary Leader," in *Black Leaders of the Nineteenth Century*, that Nat Turner's political motivations contained a core of African religious beliefs and practices. According to Wood, Nat Turner, like many first generation African Americans, was the "joint product of Christian and non-Christian cultures. . . it was the interweaving of the two over time into a single significant braid that gave Nat Turner his unusual perspective and intense vision."[3] Yet, Wood's declaration has not been thoroughly pursued. Moreover, Mechal Sobel has documented, in *Trabelin' On: The Slave Journey to an Afro-Baptist Faith*, dynamic African retentions in Virginia during slavery. The problem has been that scholars on one side of the discourse concerning slavery during Nat Turner's era discuss African retention and scholars on the other side of the discourse talk about Turner's revolt but the two sides rarely meet. This essay will attempt to create a synthesis of the two discourses. In addition, this essay is an attempt to further explore Wood's and Sobel's recognition of

African influences on Turner by reexamining these influences as primary sources of the revolt.

Many scholars recognize that Turner's religious visions fueled his revolt. However, they frequently fail to acknowledge the influence of African retentions on his visions and on his subsequent political actions. This essay examines Nat Turner and the revolt by employing Thomas R. Gray's *Confessions* and accounts of Nat Turner's visions to show that Turner not only relied on revelations in an African Christian manner but also utilized divination in a pre-Christian African religious manner. The purpose of this analysis will be to demonstrate that Turner's ideology manifested significant African religious retentions, reflecting a tense balance between traditional African and Christian religious aspects. His revolt is seen here as an attempt to reconcile this tension. In addition, this approach will display why understanding Nat Turner's complex and dynamic religious background is important to understanding both him and the revolt he led. This unique approach to studying Nat Turner and the revolt asserts the value of new critical approaches to the subject that more thoroughly explore the historical and religious milieu from which Nat Turner emerged.

Considering the abundance of works that have been written on Nat Turner and the revolt, one could make the suggestion that the discussion of Nat Turner and the revolt has been exhausted. I, however, argue that there is still room for reanalysis. For example, scholar Michael Johnson recently published an article entitled, "Denmark Vesey and His Co-Conspirators." In the article, Johnson convincingly argues that Denmark Vesey did not organize a rebellion but rather he was a victim of a conspiracy orchestrated by the mayor of Charleston, S.C., James Hamilton Jr., to discredit his political rival Governor Thomas Bennett Jr. and to advance his own career.[4]

Johnson relied on the court transcripts of the Vesey trial unlike most historians before him who relied on the Official Record Report. These findings helped him to combat the scholarship of three recent works on Denmark Vesey, one of which, as a result of Johnson's research, has been taken out of print by the University of North Carolina Press.[5] Michael Johnson shows that discussion of historical events is never conclusive. This essay is written in this spirit and hopes to provide a new approach to the discourse on Nat Turner and the revolt.

The fall of 1831 in Southampton County, Virginia, is arguably the most controversial time period in the region's history. Nat Turner, a well-known religious enslaved man of the area, led a revolt against slaveholders and the institution of slavery. A band of approximately sixty slaves brutally murdered and maimed almost every white person they encountered during the revolt. In the middle of the night, these slaves ambushed their sleeping enemies, slaughtering entire households, even infants.

Nat Turner's religious conditioning and upbringing were extremely complex. In addition to the Euro-Christian education he received, he also received an African religious education from his African-born grandmother and mother who instilled in him an African "understanding of the way the world worked."[6] The substance and intricacies of African Christianity and pre-Christian African religions in slave culture, which have an indelible place in the formation of Nat Turner, are frequently undervalued. In order to comprehend African Christianity, one must understand its dynamics, which incorporated both Euro-Christian and traditional African approaches to revelations. African Christianity is a form of Christianity in that Africans and enslaved Afro-Americans accepted and accorded status and worship to a series of revelations by Christian saints. However, the way these Euro-Christian revelations interacted with and were validated in relationship to traditional African religious beliefs determined the nature of African

Christianity. According to John Thornton, in order to fully understand African Christianity and its role in slave culture, one must understand "the dynamic elements (revelations) rather than the more stable ones (cosmologies)."[7] African Christianity can best be described as the complex exchange, examination, and evaluation of revelations conducted by African Christians.

Understanding the background of pre-Christian African religion will further explain why the aforementioned exchange was possible. Pre-Christian African religion does not rely upon sacred books or scriptures. Rather, the religion is transmitted orally and recorded in the history, hearts, and experiences of the people. African religion is pragmatic and realistic and is applied to situations as the need occurs. It is handed down from generation to generation. Changes may be brought about by necessity, whereas practitioners change what is necessary to suit their situation.[8]

Divination and religious leadership are the most significant aspects of African religion that relate to Nat Turner. Divination is the act of studying nature and events to foretell future events or reveal occult knowledge. A diviner conducts formal and informal acts of worship and attends to the needs of the community. Normally, diviners receive revelations through visions and dreams and are usually loners.[9] Moreover, they consult "spirits" to cure sickness and solve problems in the community.[10] Religious leaders are equally important as those who practice divination and some occupy both roles. Religious leaders embody the presence of God, the beliefs of the people, as well as their moral values. They are wise, intelligent, and talented, and have outstanding abilities and personalities.[11] Nat Turner embodied all of these qualities and frequently performed the role of diviner and religious leader in a conventional African sense.

John S. Mbiti documents, in *Introduction to African Religion*, that those Africans who converted to Christianity retained many of their

African religious beliefs:

> Even when people are converted from African Religion to another religion, they retain many of their former beliefs since it is hard to destroy beliefs. Some of the beliefs in African Religion are like beliefs in other religions, but some are completely different. Beliefs have a lot of influence on people. . . Therefore, it is good to understand people's beliefs well, because it is these beliefs which influence their behavior.[12]

As a result, the religious lives of those who converted shows evidence of both African religious beliefs and Christian theology. Both sets of beliefs influenced Nat Turner's behavior. This is why understanding his religious background and conditioning is so important to understanding him and his actions in the revolt.

In Virginia, enslavement of Africans consisted of concentrating Africans of various ethnicities into three regions of the state. Historian M. Thomas J. Deschi-Obi has documented that, "differential regional import patterns combined with planter preferences created three ethnic zones in Virginia."[13] Historian Douglas Chambers has established that, "[t]he concentration of Igbo (and to a lesser extent, of Western Bantu) slaves in the central Piedmont, of Mande/Malinke slaves in the Northern Neck, and of Akan/Akan-influenced slaves in the Lower Peninsula laid the foundations for the development of distinct African subcultures in Virginia."[14] Sobel has documented that the enslaved population in North America merged their religious differences to form a joint cosmology that she entitles, "The Enslaved African/American Sacred Cosmos," that was neither Christian nor like any particular African cosmology.[15] Michael Gomez has noted that the majority of the enslaved population in Virginia not only continued to practice African religions, but many of this majority "developed modifications, innovations, and syncretisms in African religious traditions on America soil."[16]

How have historians failed to acknowledge Nat Turner's African religious background? Historian Kenneth Greenberg has noted:

> The comments that he would become a prophet or that he was unfit for slavery, marks on his head and chest, his ability to read without being taught, and finally the revelation instructing him to seek the kingdom of Heaven— these signs all seemed to point in a single direction: God had commanded him to lead his people in a great battle against slavery.[17]

Greenberg is correct in this respect, but at the same time, he simplifies Nat Turner and his situation.

Turner's apocalypticism has wrapped scholars in a tight web, which understandably makes it easier for many to only see Turner in a Euro-Christian light. If Nat Turner were not so messianic, scholars would have the incentive to locate his Africanisms. Viewing Nat Turner through the lens of both African Christian and pre-Christian African religions will allow scholars to see beyond Turner's apocalypticism and deep messianic faith. Scholars will become aware that, in addition to Turner's synthesis of African Christianity, he also incorporates a pre-Christian African religious belief. As aforementioned, these two religious aspects were always modifying each other in the enslaved communities in Virginia, as well as in Nat Turner. The dialogue between African Christianity and pre-Christian African religions constructed Turner's identity.

Turner relied upon both divination in a pre-Christian African religious manner and his African Christian background to interpret his revelations. For instance, Turner states that in his first revelation, which occurred sometime during the early 1820s, a "spirit" appeared to him and stated, "Seek ye the kingdom of Heaven and all things shall be added unto you."[18] Although Turner saw this as a Christian spirit, the idea that a revelation is caused by being visited by a spirit and the belief that living humans can have contact with spirits is common in almost all African religions. Voodoo is one example. Although Turner rejected Voodoo, he embraced the belief of having contact with spirits in an overtly Voodoo or pre-Christian African religious manner.[19]

Another example of Turner's revelations is discussed in the *Confessions* when Nat Turner states:

> [F]or the avowed purpose of serving the Spirit more fully—it appeared to me, and reminded me of the things it had already shown me, and that it would then reveal to me the knowledge of the elements, the revolution of the planets, the operation of tides, and changes of the seasons.[20]

He adds that after this revelation he received the "true knowledge of faith" and he was "made perfect."[21] Turner's statement reflects a uniquely African religious ideology. The wisdom that Turner refers to is a mirror image of the beliefs of the Dogon, for whom as Sobel notes, "spirit provided a full knowledge of all natural phenomena."[22] Marcel Griaule has documented that, "in African societies which have preserved their traditional organizations the number of persons who are trained in this knowledge is quite considerable."[23] The idea of Nat Turner having been trained in this manner is likely considering that the majority of the enslaved population in Virginia continued to practice African religions.[24]

Nat Turner also claimed to have healed and brought about the conversion of a white man named Ethelred T. Brantley, who was bleeding from his skin. To demonstrate his spirit power as a prophet, Turner proclaimed that he cured Mr. Brantley by fasting and praying for nine days. Sobel points out that this is the same number of days, "used by Voudouists prior to initiation."[25] Moreover, in accordance with Mbiti's explanation of how trained diviners used divination, Turner relied on the use of spirit as used in divination "to help in the diagnosis of diseases and problems and their cure or solution."[26] Turner clearly used African divination as a healing tool in much the same way it had been used in African societies.

Before Nat Turner made up his mind that he was going to lead a revolt, the two religions were in conflict within him and the enslaved Virginia community. Therefore, the revolt could be posited as a result of the unbearable crisis and tension between African Christianity and pre-Christian African religion. These tensions were present in Turner and his community and affected them along with the dehumanization of being enslaved. Once he decided to go through with the revolt, his two religious aspects reinforced each other and became explosive. Yes, it is true that he chose African Christianity over traditional African religion. However, as previously mentioned and demonstrated by Greenberg, African Christianity failed Turner under the structure of slavery. This forced him to also rely upon the acts of divination that were taught to him by his mother and grandmother. And, as John S. Mbiti established, those who converted to Christianity did not and could not abandon their pre-Christian African beliefs. More importantly, every time Turner tried to reject his traditional African religious beliefs, they would return with more intensity. The number of his revelations grew and he increasingly relied on African Christianity to interpret them. Nat Turner and his community were in an untenable situation. They could only openly practice the religion approved by slaveholders. Thus, Turner concluded that the slaveholder had to be slain to resolve the religious struggle within himself and the community:

> He envisioned "white spirits and black spirits engaged in battle, and the sun was darkened;" he discovered "drops of blood on the corn as though it were dew from heaven;" and he "found on the leaves in the woods hieroglyphic characters, and numbers, with the forms of men in different attitudes, portrayed in blood." Finally, the Spirit visited him once again and "said the Serpent was loosened, and Christ had laid down the yoke he had borne for the sins of men, and that [he] should take it on and fight against the Serpent..."[27]

These revelations contain European Biblical symbolism but also contain a core of African religious aspects. Thus, Turner concluded that the synthesis of the two religious aspects could not be confirmed in the community or within himself if slaveholders and their coercive interpretations of Christianity were present. Liberal political theorists have analyzed the revolt as simply an attempt at liberation. If scholars look more closely, they would see that Turner had a deeper understanding of what freedom meant. To Turner, freedom involved asserting the authority to be himself without having to choose between the two religious aspects that defined him. As a free individual, he could honor both religious aspects.

Nevertheless, Turner's two religious aspects, though in conflict, could not work without each other. It is neither Turner's affective pre-Christian African religious worldview nor his African Christian worldview that influenced him to revolt. Rather, it is the two religious aspects working both together and against each other simultaneously that make Turner truly revolutionary. When examining Nat Turner and the revolt, it is imperative that scholars look beyond the obvious monolithic white versus black conflict and its role in the perpetuation of oppression. Nat Turner's revolt was comprised of differentiations, pre-Christian African religions and African Christianity. If scholars reevaluate Turner's visions and the *Confessions* under this microscope, they will undoubtedly notice that Nat Turner's visible African Christian aspects (revelations) pushed him and his pre-Christian African religious aspects (divinations) pulled him to his solution, which was to revolt. Turner's emphasis on the relationship between natural and spiritual revelations is distinctly African in its origins.

I have argued that before one can attempt to analyze Nat Turner, one must acknowledge that his religious background consisted of the merger of African Christianity and pre-Christian African religions. I have attempted to unravel the braid created by this merger in order to examine Turner's religious background, conditioning, and upbringing and to demonstrate how Nat Turner's revolt was an attempt to reconcile the tension between these religious aspects within himself and the community, as well as an overtly political action. Examination of Nat Turner's attempt at religious reconciliation is a fresh approach to the discourse on Nat Turner and the revolt.

ENDNOTES

[1] This essay is not presented in its entirety but rather is provided as an extremely condensed version of a lengthy article. The entire article will be published in the near future.

[2] Sterling A. Brown, "Remembering Nat Turner," in *The Collected Poems of Sterling A. Brown*, ed. Michael S. Harper (Chicago: TriQuarterly Books, 1980), 210.

[3] Peter H. Wood, "Nat Turner: The Unknown Slave As Visionary Leader." In *Black Leaders of the Nineteenth Century*, eds. Leon Litwack and August Meier (Urbana: University of Illinois Press, 1988), 40.

[4] Michael P. Johnson, "Denmark Vesey and His Co-Conspirators," *William and Mary Quarterly* v58 no.4, 915 (October 2001).

[5] Joe Wiener, "Denmark Vesey: A New Verdict—A Historian Questions Whether He Led A Slave Revolt, But His Heroism Stands," *The Nation* v274 no.9, 21 (March 11, 2001).

[6] Wood, 40.

[7] John Thornton, *Africa and Africans in the Making of the Atlantic World, 1400-1800*, (Cambridge: Cambridge University Press, 1998), 254.

[8] John S. Mbiti, *Introduction to African Religion* (London: Heinemann International Literature and Textbooks, 1991), 17.

[9] *Ibid.*, 68.

[10] *Ibid.*, 127.

[11] *Ibid.*, 153.

[12] *Ibid.*, 29.

[13] M. Thomas J. Deschi-Obi, "Engolo: Combat Traditions in African and African Diaspora History" (Ph.D. diss., University of California, Los Angeles, 2000), 135.

[14] Douglas Chambers, "He Gwine Sing He Country: Africans, Afro-Virginias, and the Development of Slave Culture in Virginia, 1690-1810" (Ph.D. diss., University of Virginia, 1996), 285-287.

[15] Mechal Sobel, *Trabelin' On: The Slave Journey to an Afro-Baptist Faith* (Princeton, Princeton University Press, 1979), 58-75.

[16] Michael Gomez, *Exchanging Our Country Marks: The Transformation of African Identities in the Colonial and Antebellum South* (Chapel Hill: University of North Carolina Press, 1998), 254.

[17] Kenneth S. Greenberg, ed. *The Confessions of Nat Turner and Related Documents* (New York: Redford Books of St. Martin's Press, 1996), 2.

[18] Taken from *The Confessions of Nat Turner and Related Documents:* "Matthew 6:33" in *Holy Bible.* "But seek ye first the kingdom of God, and his righteousness; and all things shall be added unto you."

[19] Sobel, 223.

[20] Greenberg, 47.

[21] *Ibid.*, 47.

[22] Sobel, 163.

[23] Marcel Griaule, *Conversations with Ogotemmeli: An Introduction to Dogon Religious Ideas* (London: Oxford University Press, 1965), xiv.

[24] Gomez, 254.

[25] Sobel, 164.

[26] Mbiti, 127.

[27] Greenberg, 3.

BIBLIOGRAPHY

Brown, Sterling A. "Remembering Nat Turner." In *The Collected Poems of Sterling A. Brown*, edited by Michael S. Harper. Chicago: TriQuarterly Books, 1980.

Chambers, Douglas. "He Gwine Sing He Country: Africans, Afro-Virginians, and the Development of Slave Culture in Virginia, 1690-1810." Ph.D. diss., University of Virginia, 1996.

Deschi-Obi, M. Thomas J. "Engolo: Combat Traditions in African and African Diaspora History." Ph.D. diss., University of California, Los Angeles, 2000.

Gomez, Michael. *Exchanging Our Country Marks: The Transformation of African Identities in the Colonial and Antebellum South.* Chapel Hill: University of North Carolina Press, 1998.

Greenberg, Kenneth S., ed. *The Confessions of Nat Turner and Related Documents.* New York: Redford Books of St. Martin's Press, 1996.

Griaule, Marcel. *Conversations with Ogotemmeli: An Introduction to Dogon Religious Ideas.* London: Oxford University Press, 1965.

Johnson, Michael P. "Denmark Vesey and His Co-Conspirators," *William and Mary Quarterly*, v58 no.4 (October 2001).

Mbiti, John S. *Introduction to African Religion.* London: Heinemann International Literature and Textbooks, 1991.

Oates, Stephen B. *The Fires of Jubilee: Nat Turner's Fierce Rebellion.* New York: Harper and Row, Publishers, 1975.

Sobel, Mechal. *Trabelin' On: The Slave Journey to an Afro-Baptist Faith.* Princeton: Princeton University Press, 1979.

Thornton, John. *Africa and Africans in the Making of the Atlantic World, 1400-1800.* Cambridge: Cambridge University Press, 1998.

Tragle, Henry Irving, ed. *The Southampton Slave Revolt of 1831: A Compilation of Source Material.* Amherst: University of Massachusetts Press, 1971.

Wiener, Joe. "Denmark Vesey: A New Verdict—A Historian Questions Whether He Led A Slave Revolt, But His Heroism Stands," *The Nation* v274 no.9 (March 11, 2001).

Wood, Peter H. "Nat Turner: The Unknown Slave As Visionary Leader," in *Black Leaders of the Nineteenth Century,* eds. Leon Litwack and August Meier. Urbana: University of Illinois Press, 1988.

AFROS AND MICS

ROBERT BAKER, III

Thus Enters Hip-hop

It was in an era of political inactivity and governmental repression that the cultural phenomenon of hip-hop became the voice of black working-class youth. During the late 1970s, African American youth in the boroughs of New York created a form of expression that today has arguably become not only the world's most influential cultural phenomenon, but also the most important form of protest for working-class youth. It is the goal of this article to explain why hip-hop, while often times problematic, misogynistic, and self-destructive, should be understood as a form of black protest and resistance. Furthermore, after a closer examination of the role that hip-hop plays in mobilizing certain segments of the population, it will become clear that the hip-hop movement, like the Black Power movement before it, suffers from competing ideologies and the lack of ideological unity. More importantly, while individuals in the hip-hop movement have retained some of the problematic elements of the Black Power movement, it also has built upon the experience of their working-class predecessors. In short, the hip-hop movement, like other social and cultural movements, contains elements that are problematic while it also embraces sophisticated forms of political activism and social awareness.

According to an article by hip-hop journalist Ryan Ford:

Hip-hop came about through the continued depletion of resources in America's urban communities during the late seventies and early eighties. Major corporations in factory towns throughout the country were leaving to find more profitable opportunities. Cities like Detroit; Gary, Indiana; Flint, Michigan; South Central, LA; and New York's Bronx borough were left as desolate ghosts of their former selves. Those who had the ability and financial capability to uproot did exactly that. Simultaneously, money that had previously been reserved for community programs and betterment was being funneled out of the inner city and right into big business and defense spending. This, coupled with the infiltration of drugs and a police force that was out-manned, under-trained, and culturally ignorant, left ghettos across America very dismal places.[1]

Despite heightened social problems and decreased chances for social mobility, working-class African American youth looked inward to fill the void created by unemployment and the limited access to public resources. This void was filled by the cultural phenomenon called hip-hop.

In *Race Rebels*, Robin D.G. Kelly points out that those looking for the roots of hip-hop should look to the African American blues tradition; while Nelson George argues that its rise should be associated with "the physical and moral decay begun by heroin… by angel dust and then the McDonaldization of crack."[2] (Both these authors argue that hip-hop must be understood as an extension of the black entrepreneurial spirit. While I would definitely agree with them, hip-hop cannot be solely understood as a legitimate way to get "paid"). Wherever the roots of hip-hop may lie, it is clear that by the early 1980s, black youth throughout the country had embraced this confrontational cultural ideology.

The term hip-hop is a vague description of a working-class cultural creation. While few have accurately defined hip-hop, there have historically been four essential elements: Graffiti or aerosol art, break dancing, DJing, and MCing or rapping. Individuals in the post-Civil Rights era who wished to resist and protest mainstream culture and give voice to their frustrations popularized each of these art forms.

Graffiti is probably the most controversial form of protest and resistance. Kelly, in his book, *Yo' Mama's Disfunktional,* argues that the early New York graffiti artists used the city's subways as their most popular canvases. However, while he states that subways allowed "the artist to literally circulate his or her work through the city" he stresses the fact that "many young people thought of themselves as waging war against the Metropolitan Transit Authority." Moreover it is his point that "Good writers not only had to be skilled artists, but because they were breaking the law by defacing property, they had to work quickly and quietly."[3] The property that was defaced often belonged to neither the writers nor individuals from the writers' community. Therefore, the work of graffiti artists must be understood as a symbolic attack against both the government (when painted on public property) and against capitalist oppression (when painted on apartment buildings and business who take money from the community but do not offer jobs to individuals from the community). It's clear that many working-class youth paint walls and subways to consciously and subconsciously protest their oppression.

DJing and break dancing are similar in that performers attempted to push the envelope of their particular fields of expression without having been formally trained. While it is important to note that historically many African American artists have lacked formal training, it is during the hip-hop era that musical production and dance became an essential component of a radical ideology. Both these elements of hip-hop should be understood as covert rather than overt resistance.

In hip-hop, DJing has become synonymous with musical production. Without having access to musical instruments, most hip-hop beat makers have turned to DJ technology for the production of their musical creations. Moreover, the most popular tactic used by these musicians, sampling (using a sound or break found on another artist's song) was and is an attempt by these working-class musicians to control, create, and reinvent their musical environments. Technology allowed these musicians to manipulate and be the owners of a particular sound without having the resources to actually own the traditional tools of musical production. The creation of the then-new hip-hop sound is directly related to the nationalistic idea of black ownership and the control of black cultural spaces.

Break dancing is a form of dance, which, like jazz, was arguably created as a direct attempt to stop the co-option of urban culture by white America. No longer could suburban white kids easily steal the dance moves they saw on Soul Train. Whereas the Twist, the Hustle, the Mashed Potato, and the Robot were relatively simple dances to learn, "breaking in contrast, was spectacular, dangerous" and difficult to duplicate. Not only did breaking allow urban youth to maintain ownership of their dance creations, but it also allowed them an opportunity to vent the emotions associated with inner city life. According to Nelson George:

> Breaking crews, in the long tradition of urban gang culture, challenged other dancers to meet them at specific playgrounds, street corners, or subway platforms. Armed with large pieces of cardboard or linoleum, not guns or knives, they formed a circle where, two at a time, breakers dueled each other, matching move for move, until one of the crews was acknowledged victorious.[4]

While it would be disingenuous to argue that breaking was a panacea for urban violence, it did offer recreational and creative outlets to individuals who were confined by poverty, limited resources, and social inequality. And, just like DJing and graffiti, break dancing afforded black and brown youth the opportunity to resist assimilation into mainstream culture.

MCing or rapping, the lyrical and verbal component of hip-hop, remains the most overt and powerful form of African American working-class protest. Like the other three elements, the first individuals who rapped over DJ's records, did so to push the envelope of popular music. While few scholars have been able to pinpoint the first person that talked over a beat, this form of lyrical delivery became popular in the post-disco era of the late '70s. The first rappers used their braggadocio rhyming to emphasize ideas of black masculinity, economic prowess, and individual capabilities. (There is no better early example of this than Grand Master Flash and the Furious Five's song called "The Message.") However, ideas of black and working-class frustration have always been the main ingredient of rap.

Because of the popularization and poignancy of hip-hop music, rappers have become the spokespersons for the whole culture. Their stories and songs have come to represent the feelings and expressions of the masses. They have become the leaders of the "hip-hop generation" and their messages are followed and interpreted by "hip-hoppers" in the same way individuals used to study speeches and political texts in the Civil Rights Movement. While the late 1980s and early 1990s saw an increased tendency of rappers to embrace an Afrocentric perspective (KRS ONE, Arrested Development, and X Clan), at no point in the history of hip-hop has there been mass acceptance of revolutionary and Black Power ideologies. But, after closer inspection, this is not surprising. Although most rappers come from the same economic background as Huey P. Newton, Fred Hampton, and H. Rap Brown, there are several reasons why today's working-class youth have had to come up with new strategies to "move the crowd."

Unlike individuals from the aforementioned Black Panthers, hip-hop has embraced the idea of black capitalism as form of community self-help. MCs have often talked about the importance of using black dollars to mobilize the community. In a recent interview, the hip-hop artist Coo Coo Cal explained the importance of investing the profits earned from rapping into his former neighborhood:

> Man, it's tough in the streets. A lot of people out there think that they have no future. That is why everybody is hungry in this rap game. I have people come up to me on the street corner everyday. …That's why I am going to reach out. I ain't going to get no Benz, no mansion. I got to reach out to these cats and let them know they can make it. Just like people did for me.[5]

Like Manning Marable's argument associating the idea of Black Power with Black Capitalism, this type of political empowerment may be viewed as less revolutionary, less confrontational, and thus, more acceptable to today's governmental actors. But for many MCs, it has been a practical way to get their voice heard while also opening up chances for social mobility.

However, Coo Coo Cal's style of black self-help is usually associated with images of criminal activity and has therefore become a source of controversy. Stories of drug dealing and pimping are usually how the protagonists of rap stories earn their income. (They are usually men as rap has historically been dominated by male MCs.) This form of the musical genre hip-hop is usually referred to as "gangsta rap." While this subset, gangsta rap, is controversial, problematic, and at times self-destructive, and even though black and white politicians have attacked it, it has become a legitimate tool by which young working-class African Americans think that they can make it out of the urban ghettos. In addition, it is essential to understand that hip-hop has become a successful commodity as suburban (and often white) youth have embraced the realness of gangsta rap. Thus, the gatekeepers of hip-hop—wealthy white men—have increasingly commodified the negative stories of the urban ghetto. Because those rapping are more likely to get a record deal telling stories about fast cars and pretty ladies, few are willing to market themselves as revolutionary rappers. Thus, the hip-hop movement is—at the surface—less confrontational than the Civil Rights and the Black Power movements.

The commercialization of hip-hop does not alone explain why it has never framed itself around Black Power and Marxist ideologies. Today's working-class youth continue to suffer from the lack of revolutionary leadership. Due to the governmental repression of the 1960s and 1970s and the murder of many of the era's revolutionary black leaders, today's

African American youth have been effectively cut off from those that would have passed the torch of Black Power and black self-determination. While hip-hop has always embraced the images of Malcolm X and Martin Luther King Jr., many hip-hop artists have never had the opportunity to develop as activists and/or organic intellectuals. Nevertheless, individuals from the hip-hop community understand the contribution of those that have come before them. In talking about the message in his music, the veteran rapper Backbone said the following:

> A lot of us fall victim to this system man. They listened to Malcolm X and they listened to Martin Luther King. You gotta fool them two ways: you gotta look like them and you gotta be of them. And with me I'm giving a message to the cats seventeen and better. This is a system where we're set up to fail from the beginning. We set up to fall short anyway so why make dumb moves.[6]

Backbone is able to relate the activities of yesterday's leaders to his work today. This shows how greatly African American youth have been influenced by the past. Yet, this understanding of the past has not translated into nationalistic activism for the majority of individuals from the hip-hop generation.

More importantly, many rappers have developed a belief that the tactics of nationalism and black revolution have run their course as legitimate philosophies for community improvement. While this may be because of an acceptance of "rugged individualism," it must also be understood as a response to the fear of police repression. Los Angeles underground rapper Phil the Agony shows a legitimate fear of the role that the government can play in silencing individuals who represent potential leaders: "Man, the Bush family let the drugs into the country. They work on another level, on some Illuminati shit. Rule the world and so forth. It all goes back through the bloodline hundreds of years to see who rules the world. But I ain't gonna get into that because it has consequences. R.I.P. Tupac."[7]

The fears of Phil the Agony are not unique. In listening to hip-hop, one gets a clear sense that many feel that the tactics used by the government to quell political activity in the 1960s and 1970s will again be used if African Americans again attempt mass mobilization. (An example of this feeling of governmental repression is Dead Prez's song called "Police State" from the album *Let's Get Free*.) Thus, many of today's artists are unwilling to sacrifice economic potential or their lives to become the liberation movement's next martyr.[8]

Moreover, like so many African American movements before it, unification in hip-hop is hindered by competing ideologies. Many of today's leading rappers view hip-hop as a get-rich-quick scheme, while others view hip-hop as an African American artform that should not be compromised by economic success. This competition can be characterized as a split between those that want to "get paid" and those that want to "keep it real." Individuals from the "get paid" camp think in a similar vein as Chico, from Chico and Coolwada, who said the following about MCs who rap for art and not necessarily for money:

> I just think that a lot of those fools in my eyes are weirdos. I'm in to the hip-hop, MC, b-boy but I don't understand niggas runnin' around town freestylin' all day but then they get home and ain't got five dollars. If you tight then be tight but what we all here to do is feed your family and live cool until your ass dies.[9]

Individuals from the "keep it real" camp have similar thoughts as Common in his song "Doinit":

> Mo'fucker move back, I pursue rap at the pace of a New Jack/Miscellaneous numbers and shoes stack grooves rap/ I deliver for the hungry and underprivileged / Something different from these hollerin' grunting niggas… Used to break dance, it's a shame / What money do to a nigga brain / If he lose his soul what did a nigga gain?… / See shirts that say "We gotta get over"/ That jiggy shit is over, the war is on / I only want to be a soldier, I'm holding on, to a culture / Focused like Gordon Parks when it's sorta dark / For niggas that's flooded with ice, my thought's the ark / Performing warming

arts with some shit for the heart / Don't fuck with radio, ignoring the charts / I could give a FUCK what you made in a year, nigga, you wack.[10]

Although these lyrics are profane and seemingly angry, one can clearly see that within hip-hop there are individuals who are desperately trying to position themselves as the leaders of the movement. One might argue that these two ideological camps are creations of corporations to sell to different customers. This may be true. But one cannot ignore that this has not only created tension within the movement, but also has manifested itself as physical violence.[11] Like the Black Power Movement, many have argued that the lack of ideological cohesion is tearing hip-hop apart.

What, then, is the influence of hip-hop? What is it's purpose within the black community? Many hip-hop performers have been successful at transcending their economic backgrounds. Mainstream rap musicians consistently sell millions of albums. This is no small feat. Whenever individuals born and raised in inner city projects are able to make something of nothing, it should not be ignored. Yet, many of these individual victories have not translated into the overall improvement of working-class areas. Many African Americans are still poor and social inequalities still exist. While hip-hop offers outlets for some, it cannot completely erase the inequalities that exist in the ghetto. Moreover, the hip-hop movement has been unable to reconcile the problematic elements that exist within the African American community. It may be that folks from the hip-hop generation will never be able to resolve these issues.

The fact remains that, at a time in which African American activists were facing governmental repression and black communities were suffering from a lack of economic opportunities, African American youth from the nation's ghettos were able to take control over a portion of their lives and give it meaning. Graffiti, break dancing, DJing, MCing, and rapping may not have completely transformed American society, but they have been powerful tools in voicing the opinions of working-class youth in both overt and covert fashions.

ENDNOTES

[1] Ford, Ryan. "Can I Live? The Death of Charles Lovelady: A Study of New Racism and the Role and Impact of Hip-Hop Culture in Twenty-first Century America." <http://www.contrabandit.com/canilivearticle.htm>

[2] Kelly, Robin. *Race Rebels.* (New York: Free Press, 1994), 187. George, Nelson. *Hip Hop America.* (New York: Penguin Press, 1998), 14.

[3] Kelly, Robin. *Yo' Mama's Disfunktional.* (Boston: Beacon Press, 1997), 60-61.

[4] George, Nelson. *Hip Hop America.* (New York: Penguin Press, 1998), 14, 15, 60-64.

[5] Biko, Delany "Project Dreams: Coo Coo Cal." <http://www.contrabandit.com coocoocalarticle.htm>

[6] Backbone, interview by Ryan Ford, St. Louis, Missouri, 2000.

[7] Now, J-ROC. "Piece of Mind: Phil the Agony." <http://www.contrabandit.com/philarticle.htm>

[8] Backbone, interview by Ryan Ford, St. Louis, Missouri, 2000.

[9] Most of these comments are based on many of my recent interviews with various rap artists, members of the hip-hop generation, and also a close examination of hip-hop lyrics.

[10] http://?lyrics.astraweb.com:2000display.cgi?common%2E%2Elike_water_for_chocola te%2E%2Edooinit

[11] The biggest example of this is the mid-1990s East Coast/West Coast argument that resulted in the deaths of both Notorious B.I.G. and Tupac Shakur. But it continues today as competing rap crews continually get into physical and verbal altercations.

THE DIASPORIC MIND

A CSADP-SPONSORED WEBZINE

The Cultural Studies in the African Diaspora Project's quarterly webzine, *the diasporic mind*, provided members of the UCLA and greater Los Angeles communities with an opportunity to present both formal scholarly essays and informal editorial opinions about a range of subjects related to African Diaspora experiences. The webzine included academic essays on relevant topics, political opinions and updates, book reviews, music reviews, theater reviews, film reviews, interviews, and discussion boards. Moreover, it offered streaming audio/video of the UCLA Center for African American Studies (CAAS) and CSADP events, maintained a database of academic information including CAAS publications, and offered daily news stories that related to African Diaspora experiences. It also included links to all other CAAS and CSADP web pages and student web pages.

The diasporic mind not only served as a tool to showcase the talent of future scholars, but also the duel function of familiarizing current UCLA students and the Los Angeles community with CAAS faculty, thereby making it easier to build working relationships in the future. The design and maintenance of the webzine was conducted by former CAAS graduate students and CSADP staff members, Robert Baker, III and Jakobi Williams, who hope that *the diasporic mind* will become the premier website and web community for African Diasporan students and scholars.

-J.W.

BALL OF CONFUSION:

A CANDID LOOK AT "IN FEAR OF LEADING: BLACK SCHOLARS STILL ENVIOUS OF MINISTER FARRAKHAN'S SUCCESS AND THE MILLION MAN MARCH"

JAKOBI WILLIAMS

Reginald S. Muhammad's book, *In Fear of Leading: Black Scholars Still Envious of Minister Farrakhan's Success and the Million Man March*, is his side of the debate concerning the Million Man March and its organizer, Louis Farrakhan. Muhammad contends that, "The four chapters in this book skillfully document suggested points to be at least considered by those desiring more clarity and objectivity in this ongoing debate. This book is an attempt to assist black scholars and writers in taking an unbiased position when they speak of Minister Farrakhan and the NOI [Nation of Islam]." However, Muhammad failed miserably in trying to accomplish these goals. In fact, the book is, at best, poorly written and unscholarly. Rather than a convincing or, at least, persuasive book, Muhammad has only managed to craft a name-calling rebuttal against what seems like every black scholar, intellectual, organization, and group that has ever criticized Farrakhan.

Muhammad maintains that critics of Farrakhan are jealous of the positive results of the Million Man March and are afraid to lead black America because they are committed to their institutions and organizations instead of to actual African Americans. Unfortunately, he offers little evidence to back up these types of claims. In addition, Muhammad offers statistics that he contends attest to the power of Farrakhan and the Million Man March. For instance, 1.5 million black men registered to vote; 13,000 applications to adopt black children were submitted; and the crime rate declined in 1996. Sounds good, but Muhammad offers no proof or sources for the support of these assertions.

Muhammad obviously strongly supports Farrakhan's claim as the leader of black America and black liberation. However, many black scholars, intellectuals, organizations, and groups have disputed Farrakhan's claim for a variety of reasons. They argue that Farrakhan weakens his claim by publicly presenting his homophobic, anti-Semitic, and patriarchal beliefs. Moreover, many critics have contended that one cannot be the leader of some of the people, and leave out most of the people. More importantly, they contend that Farrakhan has ignored slavery in the Sudan, which is conducted by fellow Muslims. The author justifies and minimizes these critiques by insisting that Farrakhan's beliefs in these matters are in accordance with the teachings of Islam. This simplified explanation leaves the reader yearning for a more in-depth and descriptive justification.

The author retaliates against the critics by calling them managers, wannabe leaders, sell-outs, and Uncle Toms. According to the author, a manager is one whose "skills are best utilized and maximized within the context of the institutions or organizations by which they are employed." Yet, the author conveniently refuses to see how this definition can be easily attached to Farrakhan and his position within the Nation of Islam.

Nevertheless, Muhammad does make some valid analyses. He asserts that most black scholars are idle from the black community and are unknown outside of academia because they are trapped behind the politics of their ivory tower institutions. This continued divide between the campus and the community is a growing problem in America and is worthy of investigation. Again, a more thorough discussion with more cited evidence would have been useful and interesting.

All the same, the book lacks facts or evidence at almost every turn. In addition, the endnotes provided are sparse and do not prove or further any of Muhammad's arguments. Farrakhan deserves criticism just like any other black leader. Obviously, none of our black leaders can be perfect. Yes, Farrakhan has done many great things for black people, but he has also done things that deserve criticism. Muhammad does himself an injustice by refusing to look at the situation from other angles.

THE HIP-HOP SOAPBOX: PULLIN' THA RACE CARD IN MOS DEF'S "MR. NIGGA"

KAMEELAH MARTIN

African American Vernacular English (AAVE) has been a powerful tool in the African American community since the arrival of people of African descent in the New World. This variant of English was used as a means of communication between slaves. Geneva Smitherman, in *Talkin' That Talk: Language, Culture, and Education in African America,* explains that slaves "created a communication system that became linguistically unintelligible to the oppressor, even though it was his own language" (Smitherman 2000, 280). Messages were coded in work songs and spirituals, which assisted many African Americans in escaping enslavement, unbeknownst to the overseers and plantation owners.

African American Vernacular English is a distinct part of African American culture. It is one of many components that allowed people of color to create a new identity once theirs was stolen. AAVE functions many different ways within the black community. It has, in recent years, empowered the once voiceless African American youth through hip-hop music. Smitherman emphasizes that "this music has become a—or, perhaps *the*—principal medium for Black youth to 'express their views of the world' and to seek to 'create a sense of order'"(2000, 269). AAVE is the clay that has shaped and molded hip-hop music. Smitherman asserts: "the language of Hip Hop is African American Language" (2000, 271). It is perhaps the use of AAVE in hip-hop that has made it such an effective tool in reaching young African Americans.

Realizing that hip-hop *is* an effective way to reach the African American audience, many rappers have taken advantage of the opportunity to exercise freedom of speech. From its inception, hip-hop has served as a type of "soapbox" for the African American community. It has given African Americans a voice to express their displeasures with the politics that have surrounded people of color for years. Racism, police brutality, gang violence, the idea of "sellin' out" (assimilation into white mainstream society), and even the dynamics of African American relationships are just some samples of what may be expressed through rap lyrics. This idea of the message within the music is what initially pushed hip-hop into the mainstream. Hip-hop artists used their lyrics to communicate to African American youth and help redirect them from gang activity in inner-city communities. This strategy proved to be effective when other attempts at controlling gang violence produced very little results. As Pieter Remes points out in *Rapping: A Sociolinguistic Study of Oral Tradition in Black Urban Communities in the U.S.*: "the advice given in these raps often has more success than official, government sponsored campaigns" (Remes 1991, 142).

Contemporary rap artists still use their lyrics to address the complaints of the community. Lyrics may speak directly to the hip-hop audience and call for specific action. Others may take the form of a narrative in order to simply relay to the rest of the world the realities of black life in America. Smitherman emphasizes rap's function as societal commentary: "a blend of reality and fiction, Rap music is a contemporary response to conditions of joblessness, poverty, and disempowerment" (Smitherman 2000, 269). Rawkus recording artist Mos Def is one of many lyricists that employ this tactic in his music. A native of Brooklyn, New York, Mos Def (Dante Smith) has quietly been making a name for himself in the hip-hop community since 1994. He was part of the short-lived group Urban Thermo Dynamics (UTD) and was featured on the 1996 albums of De La Soul and The Bush Babees. He has been described as "an MC whose devotion to hip-hop and passion for social consciousness combine with a synergy seldom witnessed in rap history" (Rawkus Records). The song "Mr. Nigga" on his *Black on Both Sides* album is a perfect example of the hip hop soap box. In "Mr. Nigga," Mos Def discusses the reality of racial profiling, while also commenting on the trend of white people who try to co-opt African American culture. He does this through signifying[1], a common practice in AAVE.

Mos Def addresses white people who use the term "nigga" directly:

> Yo, tha Abstract and tha Mighty Mos Def/White Folks got it muffled across—beneath they breaf/ "I didn't say it..."/But they'll say it out loud again/When they get wit they close associates and friends/You know, sneak it in wit they friends *at tha job*/Happy hour *at tha bar*/ While this song *is in they car*/And even if its neva said an' lips stay sealed/They actions reveal how they hearts really feel.
> –Mos Def, "Mr. Nigga"

His lyrics imply that white people know better than to say the "N" word in front of any person of African descent since whites only allow it to be heard "muffled across—beneath they breaf" or with "they close associates and friends." Arthur Spears explains this idea of white people using the term in post-Civil Rights society as somewhat of a social taboo:

> "Most Americans know that *nigga* is used among African Americans... but African Americans take grave offense at whites calling them N..." (Spears 1998, 238).

Mos Def plays with this taboo. It is in the "Mr. Nigga" verse above particularly that I believe he employs one of the most brilliant signifiers. It is very subtle and may even be overlooked, especially by those who he is *signifying on* (ridiculing). He gives the audience the impression that for white people, using the word "nigga" makes them feel empowered. Mos Def describes how whites "sneak it in with they friends," much like teenagers who only use profanity within their peer groups as a way to defy parental rules and feel "cool." He implies that they will say it any place that they consider safe: "at the job/happy hour at the bar/while this song is in they car." The signifier is *dropped* (revealed) while Mos Def rattles off these "secure places" that will supposedly protect white people from "catchin' a beat down" (getting into a physical altercation).

When Mos Def says "while this song is in they car," he signifies on the unverified assumption that perhaps more whites consume hip-hop music than African Americans. He lets the audience know that he is very much aware of who is listening to his music. This acknowledgement of a white audience also exposes the gullibility of that audience for believing they are accepted in African American culture. White people purchase Mos Def's music and sing along to a song because they think it affords them the right to say "nigga." Spears writes about this notion of white people who are involved somehow in African American culture being exempt from the "nigga" rule. He contends that "whites who are able to function in a culturally African American way and who have established solid, trusting relationships with African Americans" are able to use the forbidden term (Spears 1998, 239). He then quickly acknowledges that "it would appear that only among younger African Americans, say those under thirty, does one find appreciable numbers who accept, under stipulation, N-use by whites" (1998, 239). While young, white hip-hop 'heads' (fanatics) purchase *Black on Both Sides* and may feel empowered because they *think* the taboo has been lifted, Mos Def redirects the joke onto them. In this particular instance, he places the dunce cap on white listeners for buying into music that is obviously *dissin'* (disrespecting) them hard.

ENDNOTES

[1] Claudia Mitchell-Kernan discusses the definition of "signifying" in a particularly African Ameircan context in her essay "Signifying, Loud-talking and Marking," from *Rappin' and Stylin' Out*: "Signifying, however, also refers to a way of encoding messages or meanings which involves, in most cases, an element of indirection. This kind of signifying might best be viewed as an alternative message form, selected for its artistic merit, and may occur embedded in a variety of discourse." See also Henry Louis Gates' text *The Signifying Monkey: A Theory of African-American Literary Criticism*. New York: Oxford University Press, 1988.

BIBLIOGRAPHY

Mitchell-Kernan, Claudia. "Signifying, Loud-talking and Marking." In *Rappin' and Stylin' Out,* edited by T. Kochman, 315-335. Champaign: University of Illinois Press, 1972.

"Mos Def Bio." *Rawkus Records Homepage*, 14 November , 2001. <http://www.rawkus.com/artist_mosdef.html>

Remes, Pieter. "Rapping: A Sociolinguistic Study of Oral Tradition in Black Urban Communities in the U.S." *Journal of Anthropological Society of Oxford*. 22.2 (1991): 129-49.

Smitherman, Geneva. *Talkin' that Talk: Language, Culture, and Education in African America*. New York: Routledge, 2000.

Smitherman, Geneva. "Word From the Hood: The Lexicon of African American Vernacular English." In *African American English: Structure, History and Use*, edited by Salikoko S. Mufwene, 203-225. New York: Routledge, 1998.

Spears, Arthur. "African American Language Use: Ideology and So Called Obscenity." *African American English: Structure, History and Use*, edited by Salikoko S. Mufwene, 226-250. New York: Routledge, 1998.

Welte, Jim. "Keep It Real. Represent. Come Correct." *Inkblot Magazine*, 14 November, 2001. <http://inkblotmagazine.com/rev-archive/Mos_Def. htm>

FAMILY AFFAIR:
A COMMENTARY ON "JOHN Q"

ROBERT BAKER, III

Despite poor ratings from movie critics, Denzel Washington's new movie, *John Q*, had the highest box office total of any movie during its opening weekend. Of course, the movie has been blasted for being "unrealistic," and Ebert and Roper even gave it the highly dreaded thumbs down, saying that the film was "dangerous." However, it seems as though American movie goers have embraced the story of the working class vigilante. And who could blame them?

While the film makes overtly critical statements about America's health care system, it is John Q's pain and desperate attempts to save the life of his child that were most poignant to those whom attended the film.

Everyone, regardless of race, class, or creed has had to deal with the sickness of a friend or family member. Many of us have had to sit back and allow complete strangers to dictate the course of action. Health care providers are *trained* in healing the sick, but we have all, at one time or another, wished that we could do more to help an ailing loved one. In fact, there have been countless stories of individuals making incredible sacrifices to ensure that those close to them "make it." While we may not all have to go as far as John Q, we all want the power to take the situation into our hands and demand that those close to us live.

The film has been well received, not because it exposes the contradictions of American society, but because it allows us to put all our hopes and our pains on the shoulders of John Q. Therefore, it becomes clear that it is John Q's ability to beat the system, the system of human mortality, that movie-goers embrace. The movie allows us to believe, if only for a couple hours, that it is possible to beat the inevitable.

CARIBBEAN QUEENS: HISTORICAL MEMORY AND FEMALE REGGAE ARTISTIC EXPRESSION

LINDSEY HERBERT

Although people tend to say that the reggae music industry is male-dominated, there are numerous women who have succeeded and pioneered their way to the top. While it is important to see women, as well as men, succeed in the industry, this paper does not examine female reggae artists in relation to the male superstars, it examines their contributions in the unique space they carve out within the larger industry and society. It is the essence of the women's music that is important; its social implications for both men and women; and the unique method and means of expression of history, culture, and social and spiritual upliftment, that warrant analysis. Despite numerous hurdles,[1] women in the reggae music industry have managed to suceed and impact people by transmitting historical and contemporary insights and knowledge via music and lyrics.

Throughout African women's history, there has been a tradition of education and culture being passed on through women, who have had a great influence over their families, and hence, society in general. There are patterns of labor division and social habits that have continued from Africa to the New World, and while the culture has changed due to the transatlantic slave trade, threads of African culture and tradition run throughout the history and cultures of African people in the Diaspora. It is through these threads, that African people are allowed to "remember" the past and relate it to the present.

Africa's influence has left a huge impact on music worldwide. There are hints of African style in all genres of music across the globe. Music has been a mode of transmission of political thought, spiritual beliefs, popular culture, and traditional life. It has assisted in educating people about Africa and its descendants, led to a greater respect for the people of Africa, and has been a vehicle of success for those who produce and perform music. Despite the hurdles of racism, and inadequate acknowledgment of the contribution of Africans to the music industry, there is an undeniable truth that exists regarding the great contributions of Africa's sons and daughters to the global music industry.

Bob Marley is the most well-known reggae superstar, but there have been many others whose message and talent is just as inspirational. Gregory Issaacs, Bunny Wailer, Peter Tosh, Israel Vibrations, Burning Spear, Black Uhuru, Macka B, The Gladiators, Inner Circle, and the infamous Lee "Scratch" Perry are some of the better known male recording artists. Although these artists are recognized worldwide, female artists have not traditionally received the same degree of recognition as their male counterparts. Still, their music has impacted the lives of many and is important in shaping the consciousness of black women and Rastawomen worldwide.

Growing up in the 1950s and 1960s in Jamaica, opportunities were limited for young women. Girls, for the most part, were not allowed to associate with boys, and often spent their days helping their mothers, going to school, and working.[2] Many young women were not allowed much freedom until their eighteenth birthday, unless they became pregnant, which was not uncommon for teenagers in Jamaica at that time.[3] The men who created and appreciated reggae music in this era attended dances, visited recording studios, educated themselves by listening to radio and news broadcasts, and spent time *reasoning* (a Rastafarian term for discussing) amongst themselves about Ras Tafari and political and social events.

It was more difficult for a woman to gain access and exposure to the musical domain during this period, yet it was not impossible, especially if a man accompanied her. Therefore, we see the pattern of early popular female reggae artists coming onto the scene via their position as back-up vocalists. Although this was the early history, women like Rita Marley, Judy Mowatt, and others quickly pushed their musical talents into the studios and began opening up the door for women in the reggae music industry.

Rita Marley's musical career took off in high school, when she started a ska band with her cousin called the Soulettes, yet she had been singing since she was a child: "From five years old. Me first stage appearance was de Lannaman's Children Hour talent show at de Carib Theater. Me was so small me sang standin' on box so dem could see me!"[4] Obviously her talent stood out, she went on to have an enduring career with the I-Threes (Bob Marley and the Wailers' backup singers), and later she went solo. Her smash hit in 1981, "One Draw," took her to international stardom and she rapidly became known as the "Queen of Reggae." Her music was political, social, and encompassed the teachings and philosophy of Rasta life and Jamaican culture.

Judy Mowatt and Marcia Griffith became well known names in Reggae music through their days with the I-Threes, and like Rita, both later went solo. Judy Mowatt continued with the Rastafarian tradition that was so much a part of Bob Marley's music, and which had become an integral part of her own life. Her music raised the consciousness of many people about the role of women in history. In her song "Great Black Warrior Queen" she, from a pan-African perspective, exalts the women who have struggled:

History should never forget those great, those black, those beautiful
All the tears we've cried and the brave who've died
have not been in vain
We've learned the price of sacrifice is very often pain
Throughout history woman have been willing to pay
At nights they rock the cradle

and took to arms by day
Great Black Warrior Queen
Great Black Warrior Queen
In history we have seen
Great Black Warrior Queen
Harriet Tubman—she led her people through the underground railroad
Amy Garvey—a loyal woman by Marcus side
Soujoner Truth—condemned the system of slavery
And the list goes on, and on...[5]

Sister Carol originally came onto the reggae scene as a DJ in the 1980s, when it was becoming easier to gain access, especially in the United States. Her lyrics have some of the strongest female, Rastafarian messages in reggae music today. While much of the popular Jamaican music is becoming less conscious, with a more dancehall style, Sister Carol is "lyrically potent," as one of her album titles will attest. She is often compared to the male artist Macka B, who takes up both historical and contemporary issues.[6] Her distinct style and lyrics have given her respect and recognition worldwide as "Mother Culture." Similar to the formal and informal roles of African women in Jamaica during slavery and the post-emancipation period, Sister Carol educates people via her music on African culture, tradition, and politics as well as herbal and spiritual healing from her vantage point as a woman. Her lyrics, as opposed to most male reggae artists, emphasize the role and glorification of the African Queen.[7] She educates African women about the history they may not receive in traditional textbooks. "Womb-man" is just one of her songs in which she articulates the significance of knowing one's history:

Woman beg yuh know yourself
Know yourself my sisters!
Woman nuh rest like bottle pon the shelf
Woman like Nzingah fight fi Africa
She chase the Portuguese out of Angola
Woman like Nanny Rough Maroon soldier
Chase the British guys out of Jamaica

Woman like Queen of Sheba rule Ethiopia
Send Menelik to Solomon him father
The same lineage of I and I Emperor
The everlasting Queen fi wi ancestor[8]

The impact of music on Jamaican society and throughout the world is great. It has been a tool for political and social expression for decades. Although its purposes as a work of art or entertainment are important, it is evident that female reggae artists take it to a deeper level by recounting history from the vantage point of a woman. Understanding history and educating the people is critical to the lives of women in Jamaica.

Music has been used as a tool for this supplemental education in the life of Jamaicans and formulation of political and social ideology. Many Rastafarians feel that the truth has been hidden and denied to black people as a way to maintain hegemonic control and manipulation and continue the notion of inferiority of blacks. It is their belief that this mindset could further destroy black people, hence, it is a priority for Rastafarians to educate future generations and to let them know that they are descendants of ancient royalty and will only return to royalty if their hearts and minds are in the right place. Music is just one way of educating, but it has had a huge impact on African people. Rastawomen's music is an important part of the culture because it complements the male Rastafarian message. The Alpha and Omega. Without female reggae musicians, black women, especially Rastawomen, would have less opportunity to celebrate their culture and recount their history and, in turn, to educate future generations. Moreover, without these pioneers, we would not be exposed, to the same degree, to women like Lauryn Hill and Erykah Badu, who have in many ways been influenced by reggae music and Rastafari consciousness. Although Hill and Badu are now part of mainstream American culture, they invoke the memory of roots reggae artists who struggled to invoke a deeper historical memory.

ENDNOTES

[1] Due to length constraints, the author is not going to examine in detail how hurdles were overcome, yet it should be noted that it was not done quickly or easily.

[2] Timothy White. *Catch a Fire: The Life of Bob Marley*. (New York: Henry Holt and Company, 1983), 123.

[3] *Ibid.*, 123.

[4] *Ibid.*, 181.

[5] *Roots Daughters*

[6] *Urban Ambiance Journal.* <http://www.uajournal.com/reviews/sistercarole-potent.shtml>

[7] The term *most* is used, because some male artists have traditionally honored African women in their music as well, and it is resurging as seen in contemporary artists such as Sizzla in "Black Women and Child."

[8] Black Cinderella Productions, 1999.

A SELECTIVE BIBLIOGRAPHY OF WORKS CITED

"African Music—Popular Music of the 20th Century." *Sunday Observer*, 14 November 1999. <http://www.newafrica.com/swahili/culture/african_music.htm>

Beckles, Hilary, ed. *Inside Slavery: Process and Legacy in the Caribbean Experience*. Kingston: Canoe Press, 1996.

Beckles, Hilary. "Black Masculinity in Caribbean Slavery." St. Michael: WAND, School of Continuing Studies, UWI, 1996.

Bush, Barbara. *Slave Women in Caribbean Society*. Bloomington: Indiana University Press, 1990.

Campbell, Horace. *Rasta and Resistance: From Marcus Garvey to Walter Rodney*. Trenton: Africa World Press, Inc., 1987.

Chevannes, Barry. *Rastafari Roots and Ideology*. Syracuse: Syracuse University Press, 1994.

Clarke, Peter B. *Black Paradise: The Rastafarian Movement*. San Bernadino: The Borgo Press, 1986.

Curtin, Philip. *Two Jamaicas: The Role of Ideas in a Tropical Colony 1830-1865*. Westport: Greenwood Press Publishers, 1955.

East, Carol. *Isis the Original Wombman*. New York: Black Cinderella Productions, 1999.

Martin, Tony. *The Pan-African Connection: From Slavery to Garvey and Beyond*. Dover: The Majority Press, 1983.

Merriam, Alan P. *African Music in Perspective*. New York: Garland Publishing Co., 1982.

Murrell, Nathaniel Samuel, William David Spencer, and Adrian Anthony McFarlane, eds. *Chanting Down Babylon: The Rastafari Reader.* Philadelphia: Temple University Press, 1998.

Nketia, J.H.Kwabena. *The Music of Africa.* New York: W.W. Norton and Company, 1974.

Roots Daughters. Dir. Bianca Brynda. Toronto: Fari Int. Productions, Inc., 1993.

White, Timothy. *Catch a Fire: The Life of Bob Marley.* New York: Henry Holt and Company, 1983.

CONTRIBUTORS

Robert Baker, III
Ph.D. Candidate, History,
University of California, Los Angeles

Dionne Bennett
Ph.D. Candidate, Anthropology,
University of California, Los Angeles

Lindsey Herbert
Student Affairs Officer, African American Studies
University of California, Berkeley

Darnell Hunt
Professor of Sociology,
Director, Ralph J. Bunche Center for African American Studies,
Interim Chair, Afro-American Studies,
University of California, Los Angeles

John L. Jackson, Jr.
Assistant Professor of Cultural Anthropology,
Duke University

Kameelah Martin
M.A. Candidate, Afro-American Studies,
University of California, Los Angeles

Claudia Mitchell-Kernan
Vice Chancellor of Graduate Studies,
Dean of Graduate Division,
Interim Vice Chancellor of Student Affairs,
University of California, Los Angeles

Marcyliena Morgan
Associate Professor of Anthropology,
University of California, Los Angeles
Visiting Associate Professor of Afro-American Studies,
Director, Hip-Hop Archive,
Harvard University

Dylan Penningroth
Associate Professor of History,
University of Virginia,
Visiting Assistant Professor,
Northwestern University

Valerie Smith
Professor of English,
University of California, Los Angeles
Professor of English,
Director, Programs in African-American Studies,
Princeton University

Damion Thomas
Visiting Assistant Professor of Afro-American Studies
and Research Program,
Post-doctoral Fellow,
University of Illinois, Urbana-Champaign

Deborah A. Thomas
Assistant Professor of Cultural Anthropology,
Duke University

Jakobi Williams
Ph.D. Candidate, History,
University of California, Los Angeles

Cynthia Young
Assistant Professor of English and Program in American
Studies and Ethnicity,
University of Southern California,
Visiting Scholar, Ralph J. Bunche Center for African
American Studies,
University of California, Los Angeles